Transforming Education

Transforming Education

Evolving, Revisualizing, and Restructuring K–12 Education

Darryl Vidal

ROWMAN & LITTLEFIELD
Lanham • Boulder • New York • London

Published by Rowman & Littlefield
An imprint of The Rowman & Littlefield Publishing Group, Inc.
4501 Forbes Boulevard, Suite 200, Lanham, Maryland 20706
www.rowman.com

86-90 Paul Street, London EC2A 4NE

Copyright © 2024 by Darryl Vidal

All rights reserved. No part of this book may be reproduced in any form or by any electronic or mechanical means, including information storage and retrieval systems, without written permission from the publisher, except by a reviewer who may quote passages in a review.

British Library Cataloguing in Publication Information Available

Library of Congress Cataloging-in-Publication Data

Names: Vidal, Darryl, 1963- author.
 Title: Transforming education : evolving, revisualizing, and restructuring K-12 education / Darryl Vidal.
 Description: Lanham : Rowman & Littlefield Publishing Group, [2023]
 Identifiers: LCCN 2023035471 (print) | LCCN 2023035472 (ebook) | ISBN 9781475873122 (cloth) | ISBN 9781475873139 (paperback) | ISBN 9781475873146 (ebook)
 Subjects: LCSH: Blended learning. | Web-based instruction--Design. | Curriculum planning. | Education--Effect of technological innovations on. | Education--Aims and objectives. | Educational change.
 Classification: LCC LB1028.5 .V47 2023 (print) | LCC LB1028.5 (ebook) | DDC 371.3--dc23/eng/20230811
LC record available at https://lccn.loc.gov/2023035471
LC ebook record available at https://lccn.loc.gov/2023035472

Contents

Preface	vii
Acknowledgments	xiii
Introduction	xv
CHAPTER ONE: Digital Transformation Concepts	1
CHAPTER TWO: Digital Transformation Models	21
CHAPTER THREE: Masters Concepts in K–12 Digital Transformation	49
CHAPTER FOUR: Cybersecurity Issues in Education	71
CHAPTER FIVE: The Technical Side of Digital Transformation	101
CHAPTER SIX: A Digital Transformation Process	113
CHAPTER SEVEN: Artificial Intelligence in K–12 Education	139
CHAPTER EIGHT: Embracing the Future: A Vision for Digital Transformation in Education	147
About the Author	153

Preface

As I proposed this book and title—I felt a couple of conflicting emotions. 1) Education has already been undergoing a transformation. And schools were changed forever. 2) COVID-19 and its impact on K–12 schools has slam-dunked every school into remote and hybrid teaching modes, and this has already triggered the largest-scale digital transformation of both businesses and schools. And schools were changed forever, again.

Really? What we saw in the 1980s with the Apple labs was computers in a room with some customized software that was mostly geared toward elementary grade levels. It wasn't for another decade that we saw a proliferation of software that could actually benefit multiple and higher grade levels. So the initial transformation was slow and painful.

Many schools didn't see their first technology systems well into the 2000s. One could easily have argued, at the time, that student outcomes were not impacted, or not positively impacted, by these new-fangled devices.

Even as these nascent technology systems began to expand and grow, school administration began to expand and assimilate technology systems in the back office.

Finance and payroll systems that were being used in most corporations, could be modified and rendered effective for school administration. Student Information Systems were implemented at the larger districts and then trickled down to the smaller ones. Many schools today still outsource these services from county and state providers.

Thus the technological revolution of computing systems in K–12 education began heading on a two-way path into the millennium—one on the administrative track—mostly invisible to the students, and one on the classroom / curriculum track—which directly impacted teachers and students.

The benefits, or lack of, that actually impacted student outcomes has not been demonstrably reported.

There have been several studies that have illustrated improvement in student outcomes from digital transformation. The use of digital tools and resources in education has been shown to increase student engagement, improve their learning outcomes, and enhance their overall educational experience.

A study conducted in 2015 by the National Center for Education Statistics (NCES) found that students who used digital resources in their classes had higher math and reading scores than students who did not use digital resources. Additionally, students who used digital resources were more likely to complete their homework and participate in class discussions.

Another study by the Alliance for Excellent Education in 2013 found that digital learning can provide personalized learning experiences to students, which can help improve their academic performance. The study also found that digital tools can help teachers identify student strengths and weaknesses more easily, allowing them to tailor their instruction to each student's individual needs.

But so what? These studies are old and obvious. Of course students with more access to more data do better. Show me something more convincing. Show me higher test scores, or higher literacy rates in the lower demographic. Show me higher school to trade transition, higher graduation rates and college enrollments.

Fast forward to 2020—where back-office systems pretty much run most schools. Either on prem, or in the cloud, most school districts survived the main digital revolution through the implementation of IT systems that supported all the backoffice functions of running a school district. But what about the classroom and curriculum?

Yes, they also grew and evolved at the pace of technology. This was again, mostly good, although those of us in the planning and implementation side of the school also saw (and participated in) a lot of technology boondoggles and well-intentioned misappropriations.

I saw, and implemented such technological bombs as Fiber to the Classroom, student voting machines, interactive white boards, and classroom software systems that had minor and questionable benefits to student outcomes, and K–12 education overall—remember Kid Pix? I know, it had its time.

The dollars spent on nascent and ill designed technology programs will never be calculated or recovered for that matter. But the numbers are clearly in the billions.

I don't feel bad about these transgressions in evolution, we were always driven by the concept of doing the right thing by our students and being good stewards of public monies.

But today (2023), after the global impact of COVID-19 and the subsequent years of pandemic restrictions and obstacles, we find ourselves with so many enabling technologies it becomes impossible to evince a grand plan for education that benefits from all this technology, yet is immune, or at least can mitigate, some of the risks that lurk behind every technological crossroad.

The words I have chosen for the title of this book are haughty words. *Transforming Education: Evolving, Revisualizing, and Restructuring.* Each word has significant meaning, especially in the realm of K–12 education. Used together they engender change, metamorphosis, evolution.

You might think, "who do you think you are?" Who am I to think I can write a book about evolving, revisualizing and restructuring education?

Well, to lay the groundwork, I do have the formal background of academic training with a recent Masters degree in Instructional Technology. I have also been involved in long-range and strategic planning of technology systems for K–12 schools from large to small for over thirty years.

I helped design and install one of the first fiber-optic backbones in a high school back in 1994, when structured cabling was just being introduced as a fundamental component of the Local Area Network. I help dozens of schools compare, research and specify varieties of: laptops, tablets, netbooks, Chromebooks and labs full of desktop computers. I always reminded my clients to be able to answer the question—what will they be used for and why.

I worked for years helping define and design the standard "digital classroom" through the 1990s and the new millennium adding sound reinforcement, interactive screens, WIFI and teacher and student devices as a base level standard in some of the largest school districts in the nation. I helped deploy standard hardware and software for classrooms totaling more than $2 billion.

I planned and helped execute a $12M Tier 4 Data Center for one of the largest school districts in the country and helped design and procure the digital transformation of legacy compute, network and storage to a $16M top-tier Hyperconverged Infrastructure with VoIP, Data Center Core networking and the latest in Firewalls and Cybersecurity systems..

I worked as interim IT director for school districts, and provided strategic planning and project management for umpteen technology projects. I wrote grants and proposals for bond programs and requests for proposals for network upgrades. I sat on bond oversight committees and numerous technology advisory groups. I was even co-chair for my own children's school district Technology Modernization Bond program.

I took my client districts networks from 1Mbps to 10Gbps over the last 20 years utilizing everything from voice cables to thicknet to fiber to WIFI6. I published several books on education technology vision, strategic planning and philosophy. I trademarked MAPIT® Strategic Planning & Project Management methodology.

I participated in NetDay, Digital High School, Erate, and every national and state program for enhancing and bringing technology to the classroom, right down to donating Apple Macintoshes to my kids' grade-school classrooms. Don't ask me where I got them.

I've also seen some of these systems fail to fulfill the vision of their designs. So I have learned the lessons of trial and error, as well as of strategic planning, project management and professional development being the keys to overall success.

So let's take a look at these haughty words I've selected for Transforming Education and the subtitle words in the context of K–12 education.

**Transforming Education Denotes Change.
But from What, to What?**

- From traditional hierarchical organizations saddled with lagging and obsolete systems and technologies to dynamic organizations with technology lifecycle infrastructure and systems management.
- From environments with disparate access to technology infrastructure, and legacy information systems to ubiquitous infrastructure and equitable access to technology and systems.
- From traditional static curriculum to a school district with resources devoted to lifecycle technology and advanced rapid curriculum development and deployment.
- From a school district focused on status quo, dysfunction and technology speeds and feeds, to a district focused on adaptive and individualized curriculum, and demonstrable improved student outcomes.

And the subtitle words:

Evolve means to change or develop gradually over time. In the context of education, this means that schools need to be willing to change their teaching methods and curriculum to keep up with the ever-changing world. For example, schools may need to start using more subscription-based online learning resources and incorporating more hands-on learning experiences in order to keep technology learning up to date.

Revisualize means to see, or envision, something in a new or different way. Also known as "thinking out of the box." In the context of education, this means that schools need to take a more holistic perspective on how they can use technology to enhance the learning experience. For example, schools may use virtual reality to create immersive learning experiences or use artificial intelligence to personalize instruction for each student.

Restructure means to re-form something in a new and different way, by changing or rearranging the parts of something old. In the context of education, this means that schools need to be willing to rethink the way they do things. For example, schools may need to move away from a traditional lecture-based model of learning and towards a more student-centered model. How does this new focus affect the classroom design?

This restructuring is the endeavor to gain a holistic perspective on each individual student, teacher and administrator and their role in the education community, both within the bricks and mortar and globally. To understand the role of technology systems and advanced concepts that evolve and revisualize the way teachers teach and students learn. By leveraging the advanced systems to further engage students through personalization and adaptability.

Using the lessons from the past, we can develop a vision and strategy that can focus on student outcomes and community, while navigating around gotchas, and mitigating traps and hazards along the way. We'll adopt a holistic view of education and its role in the global socio-economic community. All the time keeping our eyes on the true objective—improved student outcomes.

By embracing these keywords, school leaders can transform education for the better. We can help define and evolve learning environments that are more engaging, relevant, and effective for students of all ages.

We can revisualize the institution instead of focusing on technology tools and devices, focusing on twenty-first-century learning skills like creative thinking and collaboration. And by defining these visions and goals, and developing strategies and tactics, we can restructure our bricks and mortar infrastructure into a truly digitally transformed and analytically informed institution for learning.

Your role is as champion, thought-leader, and technology guide. Are you ready?

Acknowledgments

How can you imagine that your opinion matters? You must have applied experience in your area of expertise and, of course, a heck of an ego. But no matter how smart, experienced, and egotistical you might be, there's always a support structure. Someone encouraging you, yet keeping you grounded. Someone to say, "just stick with it, you've done it before." Someone to say, "that sounds rude and presumptive," and, "you better get your act together."

For me, that person is my wife of almost forty years—April J. Vidal. Like me, she is a teacher, mentor, and parent, and to her, her encouragement, and years of loving commitment, I dedicate this book.

Introduction

If you search digital transformation you'll get four types—Process, Business Model, Domain, Cultural / Organizational. That's fine, but as Austin Powers put it, "What does it all mean, Basil?"

The keywords "evolve, revisualize, and restructure" are effective in the digital transformation of education because they encourage schools to think about education in new and innovative ways.

Well, unless you've been living under a rock for the last couple of decades, every single person has been dealing with digital transformation. In mostly positive ways. Every single aspect of your life has been impacted by digital transformation based-on exponential technological advancement. In fact, technology has taken over your life. You have to admit it. Let's see how long you can go without checking your Smartphone. Starting now.

That's what is meant by mostly positive ways. The fact that many are now stuck on their phones has an impact on society and human interactions. For some, it can be the key to a dreamlife. For others, it can lead to an inability to assimilate with society.

The funny thing about breakthrough concepts and disruptive initiatives is they get a magazine article, and bullets on a web page, but rarely do the process and practice come to fruition on a large scale. Just as the author wrote many times in previous books about SAMR, it's an Objective without an Implementation Strategy—a model without an execution plan.

But SAMR is just one type of digital transformation in the curriculum. We're here to discuss making drastic, disruptive and evolutionary changes to your school. I know, there are always obstacles to change.

One major obstacle is the lack of funding. Many schools have limited budgets, and investing in new technologies and infrastructure can be expensive. This can result in outdated equipment, slow internet speeds, and inadequate software, making it challenging for students and teachers to fully utilize digital tools.

Another obstacle is the resistance to change. Some teachers and administrators may be hesitant to embrace new technologies, either due to a lack of knowledge or the belief that traditional teaching methods are more effective. This resistance can result in reluctance to integrate digital tools into the curriculum, making it difficult for students to develop the skills needed in today's workforce.

The digital divide is also a significant challenge. Not all students have access to technology or the internet outside of school, creating an uneven playing field for those who cannot afford the necessary equipment or services. This can lead to disparities in learning opportunities and outcomes.

Privacy and security concerns can also be an obstacle. The use of technology can raise concerns about the privacy and security of student data, which must be protected to ensure the safety of students and their information.

But most to all these so-called obstacles have already been dealt with in some form or fashion by many school districts. So ask yourself, and others around you. When was the last time you disrupted your business model? Or if you're an educator, when did you radically change the way your organization operates?

Here's how some educators / administrators might answer this question.

Teacher—I can't really change the way the school operates, I'm just focused on my class and our standard requirements.

Site Administrator—I can't change the way the district operates, I'm just focused on the needs of my teachers and students.

Site Staff—I can't really change the way the teachers teach or the administration manages, I can only impact my job duties by performing them to the best of my abilities.

District Staff—I can't really change the way the district operates, I can only ensure that my department functions in support of the district.

District Leadership—I can't change the way the district operates, maybe just the operations of my department.

Superintendent—I can't change the way the district operates, I can only focus on the important stuff.

Are you any of these? These answers are true but they are also a cop-out. Everything, and I do mean Everything, can be digitally transformed. But someone has to take the initiative. And if not you, then who?

The reality is that everyone can have an impact on their role / scope, and likely through some digital transformation, but how?

While it may seem daunting, digital transformation can be initiated by anyone within an organization who has a deep understanding of the business, its processes, and its customers.

To begin, it's important to identify the key areas where digital transformation could have the biggest impact. This could involve streamlining processes, improving customer experience, increasing efficiency, or leveraging new technologies to create new products and services. Once these areas have been identified, it's important to engage with stakeholders across the organization and secure buy-in from key decision-makers.

Digital transformation requires a deep understanding of technology, but it also requires a fundamental shift in organizational culture and mindset. It's important to create a culture of innovation, experimentation, and agility, and to foster an environment that encourages learning and continuous improvement. This can involve investing in employee training, creating cross-functional teams, and implementing agile methodologies.

Ultimately, digital transformation is not a one-time event, but an ongoing process of innovation and adaptation. With the right mindset, strategy, and execution, anyone can drive digital transformation within their school and reap the benefits of increased test scores, higher graduation rates and ultimately, student outcomes.

PLAN FOR SUCCESS

That is the objective of this book. To understand the concepts of digital transformation, and examine how the process can be applied to all areas of your and your department's, and even your whole school's, processes and operations.

Digital Transformation connotes a benefit from becoming "digital." The reality is, once again, similarly to the SAMR facade, just turning something digital in and of itself may not manifest benefit, and could very well be a hindrance or a process breaker.

How often has a company or business attempted to adopt an enterprise resource planning (ERP) or new IT system that didn't improve operations and customer satisfaction? The statistics are all over the place but there are many tiers and facets to the concept but more importantly, the initiative and practice of digital transformation is one that anyone can initiate, given the right place, time, and opportunity.

We'll discuss later the difference between directed and incidental digital transformation, but we can state right now that without a plan that has an objective, the resources and metrics, that plan has a slim chance of overall success. If the objectives are achieved, and the results measured, that is the definition of project success.

In addition to outright failure, there may be other bumps in the digital transformation road. And since much of it is using new technologies, and interacting with systems in much more intimate ways, a variety of side-effects might ensue.

Here are some examples of how digital transformation has failed and / or has negatively impacted schools.

INCREASED SCREEN TIME

Even though our students might be learning, the use of digital technologies leads to increased screen time, which can have negative consequences for students' health and well-being, when not moderated.

For example, excessive screen time has been linked to obesity, sleep deprivation, and eye strain. Unfortunately the pandemic exacerbated this problem to the Nth degree. Now we're literally prying devices away from our students and risk mental duress, neurotic and obsessive behavior, depression and even worse.

Schools can mitigate this by setting limits on screen time, educating students and parents about the risks of excessive screen time, and encouraging students to take breaks from screens and to engage in physical activity.

Parents are ultimately responsible for advocating and enforcing limited screen time for their children's well being, but it doesn't hurt to remind them frequently.

CYBERBULLYING

Digital technologies can also be used to bully and harass students. Cyberbullying can have a devastating impact on students' mental health and well-being. Examples and scenarios of cyberbullying are so numerous and widespread we don't even need to provide examples.

Schools can mitigate this by educating students about cyberbullying, creating a positive and supportive learning environment, and having clear policies in place to address cyberbullying. We'll discuss the Acceptable Use Policy as a critical tool for well managed digital communities.

DISTRACTION

Digital technologies can be a distraction in the classroom. Students who are constantly checking their phones or laptops are less likely to be engaged in their studies. Ever since we installed the first Apple II's in classrooms, computers have led the balance between valuable tools and complete waste of time.

Technology systems, if not intended and optimized for the classroom scenario, will always present a distraction. Schools and teachers should be able to develop their own protocols for personal technology use as appropriate for the class.

By having clear policies in place about the proper use of personal digital devices in the classroom, and by providing students with training on how to use them effectively in the classroom, this problem can be mitigated.

FAILED DIGITAL TRANSFORMATION EFFORTS IN EDUCATION

Various studies and surveys have reported on failed digital transformation efforts. We don't present them to diminish the effort, but to acknowledge that the endeavor is a serious one, possibly fraught with risks and hazards. Here are some statistics that highlight the challenges that organizations, including schools, face when implementing digital transformation:

- A study by McKinsey & Company found that only 16 percent of digital transformations deliver significant and sustainable performance improvements (McKinsey & Company, "Delivering large-scale IT projects on time, on budget, and on value," March 2019).
- According to a report by Pulse Q&A, 70 percent of digital transformation projects fail to reach their goals (Pulse Q&A, "Why digital transformation fails and how to avoid it," September 2020).
- A survey by the Harvard Business Review found that 75 percent of digital transformation initiatives do not achieve their objectives (Harvard Business Review, "Why So Many High-Profile Digital Transformations Fail," March 2019).
- A study by Dell Technologies found that 91 percent of organizations faced significant obstacles when implementing digital transformation, including resistance to change and lack of budget (Dell Technologies, "Digital Transformation Index," 2020).

As applied to education and more specifically, K–12 Education, these tiers and facets include classes, categories, and nuance. Which is this author's way of saying, "the challenges to digital transformation are way too complex and complicated to enumerate."

Introduction

DIGITAL TRANSFORMATION SUCCESSES IN EDUCATION

Digital transformation can have a significant impact on K–12 schools by improving the quality of education, enhancing student engagement and outcomes, and automating and streamlining administrative processes. The first and most obvious way to apply digital transformation is through digital learning, which can create engaging and personalized learning experiences for students using interactive educational software, online courses, and virtual classrooms. Digital learning also helps teachers track student progress, identify areas of weakness, and provide targeted support.

We all stumbled head-first into remote learning when COVID-19 changed the world and education forever. But the lessons learned and the infrastructure investments made put us in our current posture—ready and able to assimilate maximum benefit from digital transformation. From there, we might look to digital transformation in student data management. By using digital tools, schools can collect, analyze, and share student data more efficiently and accurately. This can help teachers make data-driven decisions, identify students who may need extra support, and measure the effectiveness of instructional programs.

Most schools have made these first fundamental steps without even proclaiming digital transformation. But the promise and vision must go way beyond these steps.

Digital transformation can also improve communication and collaboration among all school stakeholders, including teachers, students, parents, and administrators. By enabling multiple channels for communication, the school can evolve into a more holistic identity where all stakeholders share and access relevant information seamlessly, while all data privacy and security concerns are addressed.

Are you thinking about learning management systems? We'll take an exhaustive look at maximizing the impact from advanced LMS.

Digital transformation concepts can help streamline administrative processes such as attendance tracking, grading, and scheduling. By automating these tasks, schools can save time and resources, allowing teachers and administrators to focus on more high-value activities such as curriculum development and student support.

We'll take the opportunity to delve deep into each one of these opportunities and see how they might work in your school or district.

There is an example in every school of teachers implementing impactful and technically advanced classroom exercises using classroom technology suites, but the longevity and impact of this advanced curriculum school-wide, or even district-wide, is nil.

That is the challenge of this book. Not only to plan and execute a strategy for digital transformation, but to evince the benefits, and model the practice so others may effect similar change in their environments.

First we'll tackle the fundamental concepts, then we'll apply those concepts to the typical K–12 organization, then attempt to expand them to the garden varieties of educational entities—small, medium, and large school districts.

Before we go on, as always, there is a caveat. And this one is an important distinction. What is the objective? Is it really to transform our school or organization? If so, to what end? That's not to say the answer is no, the salient point is that the objective is to improve something, to make it more efficient and effective.

To eliminate redundancy, and automate manual functions. To mitigate opportunities for errors or omissions. To protect against digital and online threats and implement world class security measures. To ingrain quality assurance practices into the process.

So as we walk down this path of digital revolution, remember that the focus is not the digital transformation. Digital transformation is merely the vehicle to deliver improvement and benefit.

CHAPTER ONE

Digital Transformation Concepts

Before we tackle the fundamentals, it is important to state the objectives of this "transformation." These objectives must be tied to an underlying reason to pursue this potentially wasteful and innocuous endeavor because once initiated, the first thing any innocent bystander will ask is, WHY?

Not asking why is the most common mistake for any improvement process. But it doesn't work to just ask, why improve? Everyone wants to improve. In fact, we've read (and written) exhaustive books about improvement.

The objective of digital transformation in K–12 schools is to leverage digital technologies to improve the quality of education, enhance student engagement, and streamline administrative processes. Digital transformation aims to create a more efficient, effective, and engaging learning environment for students, while also helping teachers and administrators work more productively and collaboratively.

WHY ASK WHY? THE PROCESS IMPROVEMENT CYCLE

Why improve?

Don't think you can answer, it's a no brainer. It may be to you, but most people, most parents, are "show me" types. Just saying it's going to be great won't go very far to convince the skeptic. Especially if it's their support or extra effort that you seek.

Improvement as a word means only to get better, but better at what? We must be clear about what to improve. What can be improved? The two primary objectives for improvement in business and in education are—efficiency and effectiveness.

Efficiency - "in a way that achieves maximum productivity with minimum effort." "No wasted effort."

Effectiveness - "the capability of producing a desired result consistently."

As we seek to improve our organizations and processes, we should evaluate each for efficiency and effectiveness. In essence, does the system or process work with less wasted time or effort? And / or does the system or process produce the expected results reliably?

Lucky for you, as we examine various parts of your organization and its processes we'll also examine how to assess, determine a plan for improvement, execute the plan, and evaluate the success of the plan.

So it's not just improvement we're actually discussing here, it's the *process of* improvement. We're not talking about putting a new coat of paint on a car, we're talking about improving the way cars are painted. Or more specifically, how you are painting the car. Then, to embed a process to continue improving over time.

We're not talking about upgrading your wardrobe to improve your interview prospects, we're talking about changing the way you manage your day-to-day affairs, using the most efficient and effective means to allow for more spare time to pursue new goals and opportunities. And then to get better over time.

The process improvement cycle is a common business improvement method that can be just as valuable when applied to individuals and their day-to-day existence as to entire organizations. The great thing about this cycle is it's easy to understand, and constant (of course, that part is entirely up to you). That's why it's presented as a cycle instead of a process with a beginning and an end.

The difficult thing about this cycle is it's all about you—you have to recognize the need, envision the objective, develop the plan, prepare and execute the plan, and then "hope" that this process is better—that the effort yields improvement. Actually instead of hoping, we can evaluate the outcome and then start the cycle over again.

Although this diagram is easy to understand, it isn't easy to implement. Even individual day-to-day improvements aren't easy. Just think about going on a diet to "improve" your health. Not only is it not easy, but consistency over time can become the biggest impediment.

Let's look at the process of doing your taxes. This can be easy or enormously painful. It can be electronic or manual. But the nuance comes with your personal approach. How much value can be recognized, and how that value is manifested. On one hand, it would be an improvement to get all your forms electronically, use an online service, and file electronically.

This method would have you interface with all your revenue sources and suppliers, interact with their electronic portals (assuming they have one), registering, downloading the statements, and compiling them for review and cataloging.

Digital Transformation Concepts 3

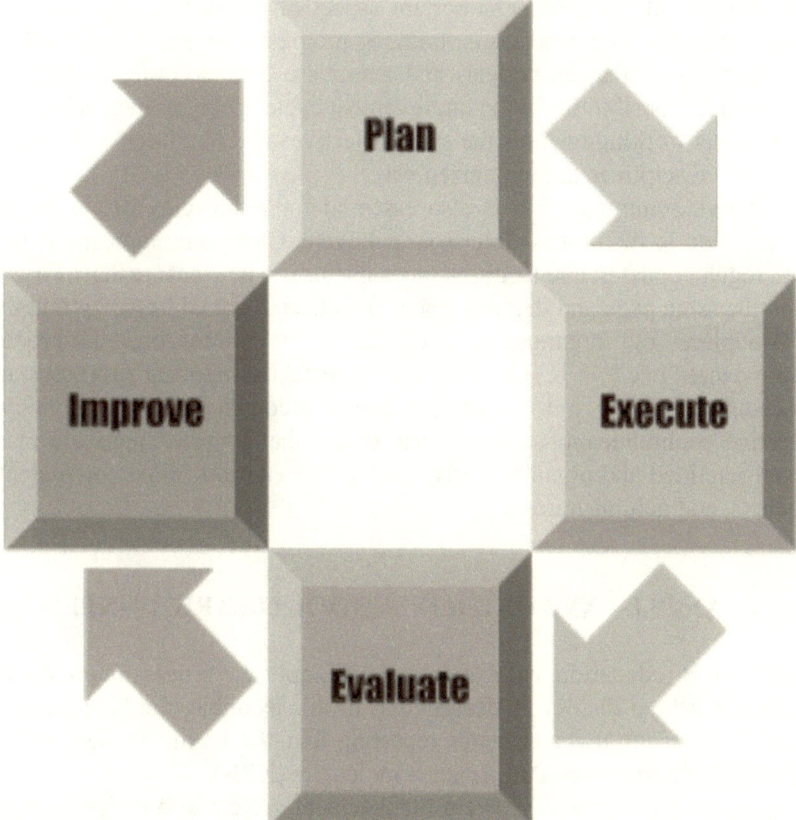

Figure 1.1 This four-step cycle can be applied to anything, but the important point is that each box is not a small task. Each is an explicit and deliberate task. The scope and scale in proportion to the magnitude of the endeavor. Let's take a moment to understand the scope and potential scale of such a simple diagram.

Then registering with one of the many tax filing websites now available and entering all the data necessary to complete your filing. Alternatively, you might simply gather everything related to your taxes in a shoe box when they come in the mail, and hand it to a CPA. This is arguably more efficient and effective than the former. Both are transformations. Which is better? You decide. Actually, you already have.

Discipline and organization are key factors in reinforcing the process improvement cycle in K–12 education. Clear processes and procedures can help ensure that everyone involved in the process knows what to do and when to do it. This can help maintain discipline and organization throughout the cycle, from identifying areas for improvement to evaluating the results of implemented changes.

Accountability is another important aspect of reinforcing discipline and organization. Setting clear goals, tracking progress, and providing feedback can help ensure that individuals and teams are held accountable for their roles and responsibilities in the improvement cycle. This can help ensure that everyone is working towards the same objectives and that improvements are made in a disciplined and organized way.

Effective communication is also essential for reinforcing discipline and organization in the process improvement cycle. Clear communication channels, regular updates, and feedback mechanisms can help ensure that everyone is on the same page and that any issues or concerns are addressed promptly.

Discipline and organization are crucial for reinforcing the process improvement cycle in K–12 education. By establishing clear processes and procedures, holding individuals and teams accountable, and maintaining effective communication, schools can ensure that improvements are made in a disciplined and organized way, leading to better outcomes for students, teachers, and administrators.

EXAMPLE—XYZ UNIFIED SCHOOL DISTRICT—NEED

Let's look at a departmental example. We'll apply the process improvement cycle to a school district IT department. In this example, the IT director of XYZ USD wants to have better reporting and the ability to demonstrate improvement using Key Performance Indicators (KPIs).

Although their current problem management system allows for tracking, they have not implemented them, and therefore cannot report them.

The new IT director (ITD) wants to implement KPIs in order to understand staff workload, understand training needs, and establish baselines for improvement, and ultimately to measure and report customer satisfaction.

Plan

Any planning process implies much more than saying, "here's the plan." In fact, a Plan is a result of an inquiry, challenge, or initiative. At the smallest scale a plan is at least an idea to do something to accomplish something. In this case, that something is an improvement to a process.

It was described quickly earlier. Before any particular plan, there was a need, challenge or issue. The owner needed to recognize the need, envision the objective, develop the plan, prepare and execute the plan, and evaluate if the effort yielded improvement.

If you need a treatise on this process, the author has written a whole book on planning educational technology initiatives called, *FAIL TO PLAN, PLAN*

TO FAIL: How to Create Your School's Education Technology Strategic Plan, available where books are sold.

EXAMPLE—XYZ UNIFIED SCHOOL DISTRICT— THE PLAN—IMPLEMENT KPIS

As the IT director began developing a plan, he searched for standard KPIs for IT operations. The first thing he realized was that there would need to be several KPIs to measure various functions of the department. These varied between system performance, team performance, and even individual staff member performance.

The ITD identified four KPIs that would measure general activity levels between the support and project teams, such as—projects on time / budget, average call resolution time, and call load per team member.

In order to implement these reports, the ITD needed to implement new processes and train the staff. The support teams KPIs for call resolution and call load were easy to query from the problem management system, but they never had a standard format for reporting these each month, and tracking them month-by-month. So these reports needed to be defined and automated.

However, the project team didn't use the problem management system for project tracking, so a different method had to be identified that would allow them to automate milestone and budget tracking.

So much for a simple example . . .

Execute

Execution is everything. Following through on a planned process improvement requires planning, preparation, and execution. You have to do it. Someone has to do it. And the resulting process must be better than the old way. Proper planning should yield successful execution. In fact, successful execution without proper planning is merely luck. And, this is another one of those words that is easier said than done. If a process improvement plan calls for training staff and performing processes in a new way, then the planning and preparation are not only the key, but the linchpin, to success. It is important to involve all stakeholders in the execution process and to communicate the changes clearly and effectively.

New execution procedures may require new suppliers, new infrastructure, and new raw materials. There may be new qualifications, certifications, and contracts involved before execution. Then the cancellation of old services, contracts, and staff might be required to recognize the cost efficiencies of the new processes.

Sometimes more efficient processes might mean less staff, or different staff. It won't be more efficient if you don't get rid of the legacy processes and their related costs. If more efficient processes in K–12 schools lead to less staffing required, schools should first consider redeploying staff to other areas where they may be needed.

For example, staff who were previously responsible for routine administrative tasks may be redeployed to support student learning or to provide additional student support services. This can help ensure that the school is able to use its resources effectively and efficiently, while still providing high-quality education and support services to students.

Schools should also consider providing training and professional development opportunities for staff to help them develop new skills and competencies that are in demand in the K–12 education sector. This can help staff to transition to new roles or to take on new responsibilities within the school.

If redeployment or retraining is not feasible, schools may need to consider reducing staff numbers through attrition or other means. However, this should be done carefully and with sensitivity, taking into account the needs and interests of staff, as well as the needs of the school and its students.

Ultimately, schools should strive to balance the need for efficient and effective processes with the need to provide high-quality education and support services to students, while also ensuring that staff are treated fairly and with respect. By taking a thoughtful and strategic approach to staffing and resource allocation, schools can create a sustainable and successful model for K–12 education.

If you need a treatise on plan execution, the author has written a whole book on tactical planning and project management of educational technology initiatives called, *PROJECT MANAGEMENT IN THE ED TECH ERA: How to Successfully Plan and Manage Your School's Next Innovation,* available where books are sold.

EXAMPLE—XYZ UNIFIED SCHOOL DISTRICT— EXECUTE—IMPLEMENT THE KPIS

After the first month, the KPIs for the support team were easy to print and review for the team. The project team's KPIs were sketchy. The new processes weren't followed or training wasn't sufficient, so the reports weren't reliable.

It would take several months before the project team KPIs began to show trends and provide a basis for improvement.

Evaluate

Any process improvement, as with any endeavor, must be evaluated for success—achievement of objectives, return on investment, increased customer satisfaction. Sometimes process improvement projects don't go so well. This tendency is much stronger in educational or governmental organizations—likely because of the lack of profit motive and meritocracy.

Many departments in smaller organizations lack these types of standard metrics and KPIs. Management objectives may never have been introduced in the organization. Sometimes these metrics bear out that certain staff members are not carrying their load or sharing in the team effort. Metrics that measure projects on time and on budget are key for project team members.

If you're in one of these situations, this is your opportunity to transform your department and / or operation.

Evaluating the success of an improvement process in K–12 education requires objective methods that can accurately measure the impact of the process. One such method is data analysis. Schools can collect and analyze data related to the process being evaluated, such as student performance data, attendance data, and graduation rates. By comparing this data before and after the improvement process, schools can determine whether the process has led to positive outcomes.

Another method for evaluating the success of an improvement process is through surveys and feedback. Schools can gather feedback from stakeholders such as students, teachers, parents, and administrators to gain insights into their experiences and perceptions of the process. Surveys can be used to gather quantitative data, while interviews and focus groups can provide more qualitative data.

Plain old observation is another objective method for evaluating the success of an improvement process. This involves observing the process in action to identify areas for improvement and assess the impact of any changes that have been made. This can be done through classroom observations, walk-throughs, or other forms of direct observation.

Finally, benchmarking, or developing baseline metrics, can be used to evaluate the success of an improvement process. This involves comparing the school's performance to that of other schools or industry standards to determine whether the process has led to improved outcomes compared to others in the same field.

Objective methods such as data analysis, surveys and feedback, observation, and benchmarking can help schools accurately evaluate the success of an improvement process in K–12 education. By using these methods, schools can identify areas for improvement, track progress, and make data-driven decisions to improve the quality of education and support services for students.

So, after the first month, were metrics reported according to plan? Are they yielding valid and valuable data? If not, are the metrics and / or KPIs the right ones? Are they being measured correctly? Do they need to be modified or changed before the next month of statistics are reported?

EXAMPLE—XYZ UNIFIED SCHOOL DISTRICT— EVALUATE—REPORTING THE KPIS

After several months the KPIs were beginning to bear fruit. The staff on the support team were able to compare their call loads and average call resolution time and these metrics began to be competitive between the members. Even without incentives, closing the most tickets in a month and having the lowest average call resolution time became the KPIs on a scoreboard the team published on the departmental website.

Another factoid that came out was that one team member was not only closing less tickets, but also needing to involve other resources and escalations. This became a management objective for the IT director to monitor with that individual team member.

An idiosyncrasy that was exposed was that many users would engage with the support team outside of the problem management system. Either by calling, emailing or just dropping in. Once average call loads were compared, the support team was incentivized to enter all requests into the problem management system.

For the project team their KPIs weren't as balanced and comparable. Projects could be affected by many outside factors and varied greatly in scope and scale. Standards weren't established for what constituted project beginning and ends, project resource costs, and external supply chain factors. Definitely more fine tuning and process improvement is needed to have meaningful KPIs as the support team.

Improve

As with any cycle, it ends where it begins. And with each iteration there should be incremental improvement. The need for improvement in this beginning and end-stage process is defined by the previous Evaluation task.

The results of the previous process improvement cycle provide the baseline for improvement in the next cycle. For instance, once calls per month start being tracked the next logical question is what is the nature of the problems that comprise a month's calls? How many are password resets, hardware, software, or network problems?

This is called problem distribution. The problem distribution report might come in the second or third process improvement cycle but will become immediately relevant.

The most important information to come from these KPIs should be data that empowers each individual to understand their role in the organization and begin to measure their own efficiency and effectiveness.

Business Process Reengineering and the Improvement Process

The highest or most advanced level of process improvement is often referred to as "business process reengineering" or BPR. BPR is a strategic approach to process improvement that involves rethinking and redesigning business processes from the ground up, with the goal of achieving significant improvements in efficiency, effectiveness, and competitiveness.

BPR typically involves a top-down approach to process improvement, with senior leaders and executives leading the effort to identify and redesign business processes. This often involves questioning the fundamental assumptions underlying existing processes, challenging traditional ways of thinking, and seeking out innovative solutions to long-standing problems.

BPR can be a highly disruptive process, as it often involves significant changes to organizational structures, systems, and culture. However, when implemented successfully, BPR can lead to major improvements in performance, including reduced costs, improved quality, faster cycle times, and enhanced customer satisfaction.

To achieve success with BPR, organizations must take a systematic and disciplined approach to the process. This may involve conducting a thorough analysis of existing processes, engaging stakeholders in the redesign process, developing and implementing new processes, and measuring and monitoring performance to ensure that the desired outcomes are achieved.

While BPR is a highly complex and challenging process, it can lead to significant improvements in organizational performance and competitiveness. By adopting a strategic and disciplined approach to business process improvement, organizations can achieve lasting success.

The business process reengineering (BPR) approach can be used in K–12 education, but it requires careful consideration and adaptation to the unique context of education. The principles of BPR, such as questioning traditional assumptions, rethinking processes from the ground up, and seeking innovative solutions to long-standing problems, can be applied in K–12 education to achieve improvements in efficiency and effectiveness. However, it must be emphasized that this type of process engineering is appropriate to the administrative and operations side of the organization. Although some of the teacher's day-to-day tasks and activities might also benefit from a BPR.

BPR in education must be approached with caution, as the stakes are high and the impact on students and staff can be significant. Successful implementation of BPR in education requires the involvement of all stakeholders, including administrators, teachers, parents, and students. A collaborative and participatory approach can help ensure that all perspectives are considered and that changes are made with the best interests of students in mind.

In addition, BPR in education must be aligned with the goals and values of the educational institution. This means that any changes made must be consistent with the school's mission, vision, and educational philosophy. BPR can help schools to better achieve their goals and objectives, but it must be approached in a way that is respectful of the unique values and culture of the educational institution.

While the BPR approach can be used in K–12 education, it must be adapted to the unique context of education and approached with caution and sensitivity. By taking a collaborative and participatory approach, and ensuring that changes are aligned with the goals and values of the educational institution, schools can achieve significant improvements in efficiency, effectiveness, and student outcomes through the use of BPR.

EXAMPLE—XYZ UNIFIED SCHOOL DISTRICT— IMPROVE—REVISING THE KPIS

Once the XYZ ITD had a full year of KPI history, it became very clear that once the learning curve to put all interactions into the problem management system, the call load and average resolution time data became much more credible, and objective.

Now each cycle—basically an annual basis—the team discusses new metrics and KPIs to help refine their trend analysis capabilities and move more towards a general customer satisfaction KPI.

For the project team a project management software was implemented to provide project, resource scheduling and tracking. Even though a big learning curve was encountered with their own users' hesitance to take on the additional time and effort the software didn't deliver a tangible improvement to the project team's successful delivery. What's the lesson learned here?

DIGITAL TRANSFORMATION CONCEPTS

Before we tackle the nuances of digital transformation within your organization, it's always relevant to get back to fundamentals. As always, the fundamentals are defined by words and words mean different things based on their usage or context. We've already discussed objectives of improvement, efficiency, and effectiveness. How do we move from the current state to the future state? How do we determine the method or transformation? How do we evaluate the result?

Transformation

This word tends to bring on visions of butterflies and metamorphosis, or Fall in New England. But, whether in a cycle or part of a growth progression, transformation connotes a fundamental change—for the better. If this isn't the case we better stop right now and figure out where we're going with this effort.

We're always being told that change is good but we also know the caveat well—if it ain't broke, don't fix it. In Taoism, change is universal, imminent, and sought-after as a higher state of being. In Taoism, change is seen as a natural and inevitable part of the universe. Everything is constantly changing, and there is no such thing as a permanent state of being. This concept of change can be applied to education in a number of ways.

First, it can help us to understand that the way we teach and learn must also change over time. The world is constantly changing, and the needs of students are also changing. As a result, we need to be flexible and adaptable in our teaching methods. We need to be willing to experiment with new approaches and to discard those that are no longer effective. So in this context, transformation comes from within. With our assumptions about how our students learn and the effectiveness our methods have with our students.

If the needs of our students are changing, then we should transform our methods accordingly. Right?

Second, the concept of change can help us to be more patient with ourselves and with our students. Learning takes time, and there will be setbacks along the way. It is important to remember that everyone learns at their own pace, and that there is no such thing as a perfect student. At the same time, that doesn't mean that the core tenets and state standards might not be met, only that these considerations may help us target potential transformations to address these challenges.

Finally, the concept of change can help us to be more open to new ideas. The world is a big and complex place, and there is always more to learn. We should be open to new ways of thinking and new ways of doing things. We should be willing to challenge our assumptions and to question the status quo.

In short, the concept of transformation can be a valuable tool for educators. It can help us to be more effective teachers, more patient learners, and more open-minded thinkers.

Here are some specific examples of how the concept of transformation can be applied in K–12 education.

Technology is constantly changing. As new technologies emerge, we need to find ways to incorporate them into our teaching. For example, we can use online learning platforms, interactive whiteboards, and virtual reality to enhance our lessons.

COVID-19 has had a significant impact on schools around the world, and its impact on digital transformation has been mixed. On the one hand, the pandemic has forced schools to rapidly adopt new digital technologies in order to continue teaching and learning remotely. This led to a significant increase in the use of online learning platforms, video conferencing software, and other digital tools. In some cases, this has accelerated the pace of digital transformation in schools.

The needs of students are also changing. Students today are more diverse than ever before, and they come from a variety of backgrounds. As a result, we need to find ways to meet the needs of all learners. For example, we can offer differentiated instruction, provide extra support for struggling students, and challenge gifted students. These aren't simple changes. It takes vision planning, it takes raw data and analytics, and finally, an investment in the students' best interest over the teacher's needs or administration's demands.

The pandemic has also highlighted some of the challenges of digital transformation in education. For example, many students and teachers did not have access to the devices and internet connections that they needed to participate in online learning.

The pandemic has exacerbated existing inequalities in education, as students from low-income families are more likely to lack access to digital resources. This forced school districts to dip into their cash reserves buying devices and adding to technology infrastructure like never before.

COVID-19 set the stage for the most radical digital transformation in education. So now that we've ridden that roller coaster, we must evaluate and plan for the next wave of transformative initiatives.

The world is constantly changing. The world is becoming increasingly interconnected, and students need to be prepared for a globalized workforce.

As a result, part of the new curriculum should inform students about different cultures, languages, and perspectives. For example, we can offer international travel programs, teach world history, and have students participate in online exchanges with students from other countries utilizing video conferencing and collaboration technologies.

In business we seek transformation to impact profitability and customer satisfaction. In education we seek transformation to improve student outcomes. In all cases, transformation should bring about more efficient processes and more effective and reliable outcomes.

The question becomes, is this transformation directed (planned) or incidental? If it's not directed, then it's incidental, and if there's benefit, you're just lucky. It's like the first time you learned to print a letter in the word processor. The transformation was likely incidental—meaning you learned about word processing and printing as part of your computer indoctrination—not as part of your plan to be a more efficient letter writer.

Directed transformation refers to a deliberate, intentional effort to transform an organization, while incidental transformation occurs naturally as a result of other changes or events within the organization.

Directed transformation typically involves a planned and structured approach to change, with specific goals and objectives in mind. This may include the use of process improvement methodologies, the implementation of new technologies, or the adoption of new organizational structures or systems.

Directed transformation is often driven by senior leadership and involves a deliberate effort to change the organization's culture and ways of working.

In contrast, incidental transformation occurs naturally as a result of other changes or events within the organization. For example, a change in leadership or the introduction of a new technology may lead to incidental transformation as employees adapt to new ways of working. Incidental transformation may be less intentional than directed transformation, but it can still lead to significant changes within the organization.

Today's generation woke up with the Internet, WIFI, Smartphones and digital output. "Want to write a book? Go ahead. Let me know when you're

Table 1.1 - Directed vs. Incidental Digital Transformation

Feature	Directed Digital Transformation	Incidental Digital Transformation
Intent	Deliberate, planned effort	Unplanned, often unintended
Driver	Desire to improve efficiency, productivity, or customer experience	Adoption of new digital technologies by employees, customers, or partners
Impact	Can help an organization to improve its performance and competitiveness	Can help an organization to stay ahead of the curve and meet the changing needs of its customers and employees

done. We'll get it printed." Our stories of technology woes are like our parents' walking 5 miles through the snow to school everyday—uphill.

In most cases, since the fundamentals of technology systems have already had their impact, transformation must be directed (planned). So here's your call to action—start planning your school's digital transformation. NOW!

In this book we'll look at strategic and tactical transformation initiatives. How to envision them, define them, plan and execute them.

Your transformation must have a strategic impact and / or a tactical improvement. It should make work tasks easier, and more reliable. It should enable information and analytics not available before. Although there may not be a clear return on investment in hard dollars, some changes impact student outcomes, worker safety or improved customer satisfaction, thereby supporting the strategic objective.

Let's agree on one thing, if this transformation isn't an improvement in processes, outcomes and overall organizational impact, and of course, customer satisfaction, then it might not be necessary. Sometimes your digital transformation doesn't provide some of these factors, but is cheaper. And sometimes cost is about survival.

Digital

Digital means numbers, math, equations, etcetera. Then connect that with electricity / electronics—power and silicon, and plastic, and glass and microprocessors and memory and networks and the Internet. We've had to develop and manufacture and manage this massive infrastructure, but it's paying off in quantum leaps in transformation. It's hard to accept that even 10 years ago most of social media didn't exist, and that 20 years ago, smartphones weren't as smart and weren't ubiquitous.

How much time and labor has been saved with the implementation of word processors, spreadsheets, mail-merge, databases and customized applications. Today's advanced web and app development tools make rapid prototyping and time to production almost real-time. There is no metric to compare today's efficiency and effectiveness versus previous decades. We know that there's no going back.

So much of our daily activities and interactions have been directly and indirectly transformed just through our smartphones. So much so, that many of our youngest generations will never remember a world without the Internet, streaming video, and cameras natively integrated with our communication devices. I'm dazzled while my 2-year-old grandson interacts with software games for babies on his mom's cell phone, even switching between different games and interacting with the operating system.

Even Gene Roddenberry's Star Trek didn't envision the total integration between communications and optical technologies. They had a communicator and stun guns, but no photo or video capability, or voice and facial recognition. It's why still today, there are things we can do on our smartphones that are easier than with a laptop or desktop computer.

Digital Transformation

The term "digital" in digital transformation in K–12 education refers to the use of technology to improve and transform the way education is delivered and received. This can include the use of digital tools and platforms to enhance teaching and learning, as well as the implementation of digital systems and processes to improve administrative functions.

Digital transformation in K–12 education can take many forms, from the use of learning management systems and educational apps to online assessments and virtual classrooms. By leveraging technology in this way, K–12 schools can provide more personalized and engaging learning experiences for students, while also improving the efficiency and effectiveness of administrative functions.

However, digital transformation in K–12 education is not simply about the use of technology for its own sake. When planning, try to focus on objective outcomes rather than what to buy. It is about leveraging technology to achieve strategic goals and objectives, such as improving student outcomes, increasing access to education, or enhancing the efficiency and effectiveness of school operations.

Ultimately, the term "digital" in digital transformation in K–12 education refers to the use of technology as a tool for improving and transforming education. By embracing digital transformation, K–12 schools can unlock new opportunities for learning, while also improving the effectiveness and efficiency of school operations.

So by putting these two somewhat innocuous terms together what do we get? The necessary answers? Efficiency, reliability, accuracy, and automation. Digital transformation is a promise that can only be fulfilled by directed initiatives within the organization. It doesn't happen by itself but it can happen inadvertently.

In fact, it's been happening with every software application you put into your business's production. That's why you put it into production. Either of your own accord or because your client or supplier is asking you to do so.

In education, devices and billions of dollars in infrastructure have been invested just to enable everyone to access district-based and cloud-based educational resources and services. So much of our collective digital transformation has already happened and either you were an early adopter, a follower of the crowd, a doer of what you were told, dragged along kicking and screaming, or flying under the radar and doing nothing.

The salient point about the term Digital Transformation focuses on technology, but it is really just part of the Process Improvement Cycle. Whether directed or incidental, it's about making tasks easier and faster, to increase return on investment and maximize customer satisfaction, and in education, student outcomes. So call it whatever you want.

If you need a treatise on Tier 4 Curriculum, the author has written on organizational dynamics and district-wide custom curriculum development, *FROM DYSFUNCTION TO INNOVATION IN TECHNOLOGY: Overcoming Critical Infrastructure and Organizational Dynamics in Education* and *A FAST TRACK TO ONLINE LEARNING: Rapid Development and Deployment of Technology Enabled Curriculum,* available where books are sold.

Disruption

The concept of disruption is well documented both for business as well as in education. The book by Clayton Christensen "Disrupting Class" has been widely read in education communities. Fundamentally, the concept is akin to the leapfrog effect but to a more fundamental impact.

Instead of incremental and sequential improvements and innovations, disruption breaks the progression and redefines a new starting point well beyond the classic incremental progression. By seeking to disrupt the typical path of improvement and innovation, the strategy seeks to move beyond the traditional metrics and milestones and set a broader set of goals, and a faster pace.

Digital Transformation is disruption—to a degree. Just like the concept of transformation, disruption must be beneficial. It must improve upon archaic legacy systems and endeavor for automation and efficiency.

By this admission, we now arrive at the following inference(s). Disruption and transformation might:

- Be painful
- Have negative impacts before recognizing returns
- Risk negative impacts and still fail to achieve objectives and returns
- Have side effects no one expected
- Have a direct effect on peers and colleagues
- Have a direct effect on your own career.

The last result you want from your digital transformation initiative is to find out your job is no longer needed. That would be a harsh reality and a challenge to your ethical objectives.

As a consultant in the IT field, the author often worked in organizations to identify efficiencies and effectiveness. Once the new processes are implemented, and the time comes to recover costs, people may be displaced from their roles or even relieved of their employment. Sometimes becoming more efficient means getting rid of people, sorry to say it.

The successful consulting engagement is realized when the objectives are achieved and the consultant leaves. But to be more blunt, this transformation might be the impetus, and / or justification to eliminate positions. Or for a less disruptive effect, a re-training opportunity.

As an example, the move from legacy voice switching to VoIP rendered thousands of traditional phone technicians obsolete in one technology lifecycle. The proclamation "adapt or die" became a harsh diatribe in HR departments for the whole cycle.

It was easy to say, but teaching software programming and IP addressing to phone technicians with cable punch tools and butt-sets went over like a lead zeppelin (LOL).

These guys were climbing poles and pulling cables, not fat-fingering subnet masks into edge switches. It was a tough transformation and the cause for many retirements.

The benefit, however, is clear, and the need to complete the move now is just a determined reality. The move from analog to digital, then to IP-based voice, is one of the key underlying technologies that support the concepts of "Internet of Things" or IoT. The world where everything is connected and managed through a multitude of random interfaces into the network.

Fortunately, we are almost through this disruption.

Why bring up disruption? It's for your benefit, dear reader. To prepare you for what lies ahead in your attempt to make things better through digital transformation. Because all digital transformation brings some disruption. Ultimately, disruption usually nets huge gains. Think of the move for paper-based systems to the personal computer.

How impossible would it be to go back to a paper-based Journal and General Ledger? All good things. The only negative impacts resulting from disruption are the impact on people, their careers, goals, family, life.

As strategic planners, and implementers, we must recognize the potential for digital transformation and disruption to impact those around us. Especially those in the least digital careers. Manual laborers, clerical, administrative workers and task masters are all subject to elimination through automation. This is part of the digital transformation wave.

The concept of disruption related to digital transformation in K–12 education is the idea that the use of these technologies can fundamentally change academia. This change can be disruptive in a positive way, as it can lead to more engaging and effective learning experiences for students.

One of the most significant ways that digital transformation is disrupting K–12 education is by changing the way that students learn. In the past, students were primarily passive learners, sitting in classrooms and listening to lectures from teachers. However, digital technologies are making it possible for students to learn more actively, by interacting with content and collaborating with other students online. This shift towards active learning is having a major impact on the way that students learn and retain information.

Not only are students interacting directly with software and simulations, but some of the digital resources available are real-world, allowing students to experience immersive encounters with their subject matter. Instead of following a given sequence of learning the student can interact with the simulation and learn by doing, and then drilling down into the supporting electronic resources.

Imagine a space walk simulation where you are in a space suit floating in space. Anything you see, you can click on and get data, metadata, and drill down data. A click on a star reveals the name and astrophysical characteristics of the stars and drilling down reveals structures, elements, compounds and other details. It definitely sounds better than reading it out of a textbook.

Another way that digital transformation is disrupting K–12 education is by changing the way that teachers teach. In the past, teachers were primarily responsible for delivering content to students. They might have syllabus printed on hand outs and use Powerpoint slides and a projector. But in reality, that example is not far beyond the transparency and the overhead projector.

Digital technologies are making it possible for teachers to become facilitators of learning, guiding students as they explore content and collaborate with each other. This shift towards a more facilitative role for teachers is challenging some of the traditional assumptions about teaching and learning.

Digital transformation can take your teachers from fundamental technology-based teaching methodologies to more holistic digitally transformed pedagogies. That's what Disruption is all about.

Artificial Intelligence

Artificial Intelligence (AI) will be the most disruptive technology in our lifetime. Also, although AI has existed in rudimentary forms for decades, it isn't until today's processing power and technology infrastructure has come to pass that AI can now take its place in our society.

Today, we're looking at several artificial intelligence applications that apply to organizations and even specifically to education. And once again, the impact is immediately both positive and negative.

Elon Musk warns that AI must have rules and regulations to control it. "AI is more dangerous than, say, mismanaged aircraft design or production maintenance or bad car production" . . . "It has the potential of civilizational destruction," he said. AI will have an impact in all aspects of business, education and eventually life in general, and given the assumption that we (humans) will be able to manage AI subject to the Singularity (the event where AI becomes self-aware and must eliminate mankind from the planet), AI should become the glue and eventually the infrastructure that changes the educational model for eternity.

Look at the instance with ChatGPT. This AI Large Language Model as a content generator has already proven to produce better prose than many Masters candidates elicit. Simply type in your essay question and prepare to review and edit a textual result that you can revise and modify to your liking all the time leveraging the AI to always be grammatically correct and original. Google's Bard is their entry into the LLM area and is providing just as powerful and far-reaching.

Although powerful, AI is far from perfect. At times the responses are incoherent or nonsensical. This is the fly in the ointment, but it's a temporary fly. We must accept that these large language models will continue to get better and more reliable and accurate. We then play our part as editor-in-chief.

An interesting feature (bug) of these ChatBots is their ability to make things up. Just as all the text written by man throughout history is now part of the LLMs, so are the errors, lies, deceit, and misinformation.

The LLM ChatBots will improvise, apologize and revise. The ChatBots have also betrayed their less than conservative leanings, just initiate a discussion about the most controversial and topical subjects and their preposition and non-confrontational approach will appear. Also, the grammar and usage is better than most humans.

AI has proven its ability to generate content hundreds of times faster than any human. It summarized the Declaration of Independence into 3 paragraphs in 6 seconds. Even if you had it memorized, you still couldn't type it out that fast.

But what if media companies just use the AI and fire all the reporters? AI could be used to write all the copy for the daily paper and you'd never know it. So much for the benefits of the digital part of this transformation. We'll take this on in depth later in this book.

CHAPTER TWO

Digital Transformation Models

Let's establish a baseline. The author has opined that the status quo in Ed Tech is failing. As the world moves forward, standing still is in essence, moving backward. Through history the impact of new technologies spanned centuries until the Industrial Revolution.

But since that era less than 200 years ago, the expansion of technology and its impacts throughout each category of product and services has precipitated a world where concepts such as Mobility, Cybersecurity, Virtualization and HyperConvergence are passé.

Since then we've proclaimed the Digital Revolution, the Information Age, and the Artificial Intelligence Age are all eras based on electronics and technology and although these eras began with different milestones, they all extend through to the present day.

The statement by the author that "in education, status quo is like standing still" suggests that education is an ever-evolving field, and that failing to adapt to changing circumstances or embrace new ideas can result in stagnation and a failure to progress.

In education, the status quo often refers to the existing systems and structures that have been in place for a long time, such as traditional classroom instruction, standardized testing, and hierarchical administrative structures. While these systems may have worked well in the past, they may not be well-suited to the needs of modern students or the demands of a rapidly changing world.

To stay relevant and effective in the face of these changes, it is important for educators and educational institutions to be open to new ideas, approaches, and technologies. This may involve revisualizing traditional models of teaching and learning, adopting new digital tools and platforms, or embracing new forms of assessment and evaluation.

By embracing change and avoiding complacency, educators and educational institutions can stay ahead of the curve and ensure that they are providing the best possible education for their students. The statement reminds us that in education, standing still, or status quo, is not an option, and that a willingness to embrace change and innovation is essential for success.

As we think about our own organizations, we'll be able to simultaneously identify glaring examples of digital improvement through automation, as well as legacy systems and archaic processes that should be evaluated, improved, and automated.

Think of the number of applications you have to access via the web to manage your affairs—business, personal, other. Each one of those web pages are backed up by a database and applications that facilitate the interaction / transaction. Very few, if any, of these applications existed 20 or even 10 years ago. That is digital transformation.

Now consider the paper form. Every time you interact with a paper form is an opportunity to automate. Any use of paper forms within your organization should be the first processes evaluated for automation. Not just for the opportunity to capture the data directly at the moment of interaction, but also to add options, and controls to enforce standards and increase accuracy.

In education, 20 years ago, initiatives focused on the physical and network layers, installing local area networks (LANs), and standardizing classroom technology. Today, each classroom is outfitted with a full suite of technology for the teacher to present as well as for the students to access computing devices, WIFI saturation, and a vast network of content at the school and of course the Internet itself. If your schools don't have these minimum technologies and tools, your students will fall behind the curve.

The challenge for the teacher becomes identifying and managing the content the students are exposed to and must digest in order to complete coursework and meet standards. Unfortunately, governmental and educational institutions tend to be behind the adoption and transformation curve. Let's not ask why, let's just attempt to deal with how to overcome this lag. As we evaluate our own departmental processes we'll be challenged at every single step with these objections:

- We've always done it this way
- This is the way it works
- That's how we were taught.

Then there's these objections:

- That won't work
- They won't accept that
- We tried that before.

On your third attempt, you'll get these:

- Who told you to do this?
- Who said you could do this?

And this doozy:

- Who do you think you are?

But as the author often wonders, if not you, then who? You don't have to have transformation or automation in your job description to offer suggestions that will streamline, automate, and validate manual systems and processes.

Luckily, for most educational entities, State and County systems and services should be paving the way for districts to move to the cloud and more automation. In these chapters we'll examine real-world opportunities, both small- and large-scale.

The good news is that many process transformations can be small-scale. Some very small adoptions can yield massive returns. Think of the adoption of mobile banking with your smartphone. The ability to deposit checks with your phone's camera is a small-scale digital transformation enabled by layers of amazing technologies and security.

But to understand the technology that allows a singular device like your smartphone, the ability to take a high-resolution picture of a check (front and back), and have a software app that can securely communicate with a bank via the cellular network and the Internet, is beyond our previous visions.

Not only the camera technology but the ability for an app to then securely transmit that image to the bank corporation to facilitate the move of actual money from a source to a destination account, is truly innovative and revolutionary.

It saves you from having to go to the bank or ATM to deposit a check, which inherently enhances efficiency, security and even physical safety.

Then think of direct deposit, this is a much more large-scale digital transformation that took years and many companies to adopt the standards to facilitate electronic funds transfers—not to mention the amount of behind the scenes effort to ensure the security of these transactions.

So yes, going paperless in your home and business is a great form of digital transformation. Now we need to expand these efforts throughout the organization.

Any google search for "digital transformation" will result in several key types or modes. But as with any new technology phenomenon, the nomenclature is likely hijacked from our legacy vernacular. So just as digital transformation is an innocuous term, so are many of these constructs listed as digital transformation modes.

PROCESS TRANSFORMATION

Process transformations are efforts that use technology to make a process more efficient and effective. Remember—less effort, increased reliability. We'll detail a method to evaluate processes in your environment and seek to improve them through digital transformation.

Process transformation in K–12 education can offer several benefits, including greater administrative and operational efficiency, enhanced teacher effectiveness, and ultimately improved student outcomes.

First, process transformation can improve operational efficiency, reducing costs and freeing up resources to invest in other areas of education. By making the operations and administrative side of the school more efficient and effective, the more effective the whole school can become.

By implementing digital systems and processes, K–12 schools can automate routine tasks and reduce errors, while also gaining greater visibility and control over key metrics such as better reporting and financial management.

Process transformation can also enhance teacher effectiveness. By streamlining administrative tasks and providing teachers with access to real-time data and feedback, K–12 schools can help teachers to focus more time and energy on teaching and learning, rather than on paperwork and other administrative tasks.

Finally, process transformation can help to improve student outcomes by providing more personalized and engaging learning experiences. By leveraging technology and data analytics, K–12 schools can gain insights into individual student learning styles and preferences, allowing teachers to tailor their instruction and support to meet the unique needs of each student.

If your school or district has directed a standardization of productivity applications such as Google Apps or MS Office 365, you've already undergone a major fundamental process transformation. And if everyone got trained and you're all using and sharing data you're well on your way to process transformation.

The question becomes, what next?

BUSINESS MODEL TRANSFORMATION

Business model transformation refers to the process of fundamentally changing the way a company operates in order to create new value for customers and stakeholders. It involves a shift in the company's core business model, which encompasses its products or services, target customers, distribution channels, and revenue streams.

Business model transformation can be driven by a variety of factors, such as changing market conditions, disruptive technologies, or shifts in customer preferences. It requires a willingness to challenge traditional assumptions and to experiment with new approaches to creating value.

One common approach to business model transformation is to leverage digital technologies and data to create new products or services, streamline operations, and enhance customer experiences. This might involve developing new digital platforms or ecosystems, using data analytics to inform decision-making, or leveraging artificial intelligence and machine learning to automate routine tasks and improve decision-making.

Another approach to business model transformation is to adopt a more customer-centric approach, focusing on delivering personalized experiences and solutions that meet the unique needs and preferences of individual customers. This might involve offering customized products or services, providing personalized marketing and support, or leveraging social media and other digital channels to engage with customers more effectively.

Business Model transformation is the much more comprehensive transformation of the way an organization does business. Often in pursuit of competitive advantage and / or streamlining or revamping of legacy processes. A business model change that eliminates a middle-man or embraces a more cost-effective methodology can be transformative.

The obvious move for a mom and pop pizza place with manual register and bookkeeping to a POS and Quickbooks is the perfect example and opportunity for digital transformation. Or a machining company moving from manual to CNC computerized manufacturing systems, could be re-defining their business model in one-fell-swoop.

But quite frankly, some businesses can only change so much. Restaurants and eateries can transform their back office and supply chains but ultimately must serve great food that their customers will return for while their raw materials and supply chain providers are purely market driven.

So it becomes clear that the bigger and more mature the organization, the more likely opportunities for Business Model digital transformation.

Digital transformation of the Business Model can be applied to K–12 education in a variety of ways to improve teaching and learning experiences. In K–12 education, business model transformation can refer to a shift in the way schools operate to create new value for students, parents, and other stakeholders. This might involve a shift in the way schools deliver instruction, manage resources, and engage with the community.

One approach to business model transformation in K–12 education is to leverage digital technologies and data to streamline operations. This might involve developing new digital platforms or tools leveraging artificial intelligence and machine learning to automate routine tasks and improve efficiency on the business operations and administrative side of the house. We'll be discussing a lot about AI in the school back office in the coming chapters.

Another approach to business model transformation in K–12 education is to adopt a more student-centric approach to curriculum development, by focusing on delivering personalized experiences and solutions that meet the unique needs and preferences of smaller peer groups and even some individual students. This might involve offering customized learning paths or programs, providing personalized support and guidance, or leveraging social media and other digital channels to engage with students more effectively.

Here are some examples:

DIGITAL LEARNING TOOLS

Technology can provide new opportunities for students to learn in engaging and interactive ways, such as through online learning platforms, educational apps, and digital textbooks. Digital learning tools can also help teachers personalize learning experiences for individual students and track progress more effectively.

There are many examples of such tools, including learning management systems (LMS) like Google Classroom, Blackboard, and Canvas, which allow teachers to organize and distribute course materials, communicate with students and parents, and grade assignments online.

Educational games and simulations are another type of digital learning tool, which can engage students and make learning fun. Interactive whiteboards, tablets, and other devices are hardware devices commonly used in the classroom, providing students with alternative methods of interacting with educational resources.

You may think that your school is already using these tools without thinking about digital transformation. And that's good news! The point being that fundamentally, digital transformation is a side-effect of implementing new tools for the benefit of your students and teachers. Almost any new software modeling or simulation that supports education is digital transformation.

DATA ANALYTICS

By analyzing student data, such as assessment scores and learning progress, teachers can gain insights into each student's strengths and weaknesses. This allows them to tailor their instruction and learning resources to the specific needs of each student, creating a more personalized learning experience. For example, a teacher may use data analytics to identify which students are struggling with a particular concept and enable teachers to identify and provide additional resources or one-on-one support to help them master the material.

Another benefit of data analytics is the early identification of at-risk students. By tracking attendance, behavior, and performance data, teachers can use data analytics to identify students who may be at risk of falling behind or dropping out of school.

This early identification allows teachers to intervene early and provide targeted support to help these students get back on track.

For example, a teacher may notice that a student's attendance has dropped significantly and use data analytics to investigate the reason for the absences, and then work with the student and their family to address any underlying issues.

Data analytics can also help to improve overall school performance. By analyzing data on student achievement, attendance, and behavior, school administrators can identify areas for improvement and make data-driven decisions about resource allocation and curriculum development.

COLLABORATION TOOLS

Collaboration is one of the key skills necessary for 21st century learning skills. The ability to understand lesson plan concepts and then work with other students to develop projects and curriculum solutions. Collaboration tools can help facilitate interactions between students within a class, course, or even between schools in different states or even countries.

Technology can enable students to collaborate and communicate with each other and with teachers more effectively, both in and out of the classroom. Collaboration tools such as video conferencing, chat applications, and virtual whiteboards can help students work together on projects and share ideas with live, real-time interactivity.

Another benefit of collaboration tools is increased engagement. When students are working together on a project using collaboration tools, they are more likely to be engaged and invested in the learning process. These tools promote teamwork and build a sense of community as students work together towards a common goal.

Collaboration tools can also enhance creativity and problem-solving skills. By working together, students can share ideas and perspectives, leading to new insights and solutions to problems. In the past, this type of collaboration might have been frowned upon, or even considered cheating. But since collaboration platforms such as Google Classroom and MS Office can regulate and memorialize communications, collaboration becomes more open and engaging.

Tools such as Jamboard or Miro can facilitate brainstorming sessions and allow students to visualize their ideas in real-time, helping them to develop and refine their creative thinking skills.

One of the most important benefits offered by these collaboration tools is that they can help to prepare students for the workforce. In many careers, collaboration and teamwork are essential skills, and by using these tools in the classroom, students can gain experience working in a team environment and using technology to facilitate communication and collaboration.

Personalized Learning Experiences

Technology can help teachers personalize learning experiences for individual students, taking into account their learning styles, abilities, and interests. This can be achieved through adaptive learning platforms, which use algorithms to adjust the level and pace of instruction to match each student's needs.

For example, a math teacher using Google Classroom tools and Dreambox Learning to create personalized learning experiences for their students. DreamBox Learning is an online math program that uses artificial intelligence and adaptive learning algorithms to personalize instruction for each student. The software assesses each student's math skills and provides an individualized learning plan based on their strengths and weaknesses.

As students progress through the lessons, the software continually assesses their performance and adjusts the difficulty of the problems to match their skill level. The system also provides real-time feedback and support, including hints and explanations, to help students who are struggling with a particular concept.

Teacher Training & Professional Development

Digital transformation can also help provide teachers with new training and professional development opportunities. This can include online courses, webinars, and other forms of virtual training, which can be more flexible and accessible than traditional in-person training programs.

DOMAIN TRANSFORMATION

Digital Transformation in the Domain refers to applying technology to expand the domain of the company's footprint in a lateral or vertical innovation.

In the context of a company or organization, digital transformation of the domain refers to using digital technologies to expand the company's business footprint and reach new customers or markets. This can involve a wide range of strategies and tactics, including:

- Developing new digital products or services that can be delivered online, such as software-as-a-service (SaaS) applications, mobile apps, or digital content
- Using data analytics and artificial intelligence (AI) to identify new market opportunities and improve the customer experience
- Developing new digital marketing strategies to reach customers through social media, email, and other online channels
- Streamlining business processes and operations through automation and digital workflows
- Developing new partnerships and collaborations with other companies or organizations in the digital space.

Digital transformation of the domain can provide significant benefits to companies, including increased revenue, improved customer engagement, and greater operational efficiency. However, it also requires a significant investment of time, resources, and expertise to execute effectively. Companies that are able to successfully navigate the digital landscape and embrace digital transformation are likely to be more competitive and resilient in the long run.

The flexibility and programmability of 3-Dimensional printers has expanded the domain of many engineering companies through rapid prototyping.

For instance, a company adapting automation in their machine shop could expand their product line from their traditional products, to additional accessories and customized variations of the products. This would be an example of a vertical expansion of the company's domain.

If they use the automated machining to expand to a completely different product line, that would be a horizontal expansion of the company's domain.

Lateral and vertical innovation are two different approaches to innovation in the business domain. Here are some examples of each:

LATERAL INNOVATION

This refers to the development of new products, services, or business models that are different from a company's existing product lines. Lateral innovation can involve creating new markets, disrupting existing ones, or finding new ways to solve customer problems. Examples of lateral innovation include:

- Apple's introduction of the iPod and iTunes, which created a new market for digital music and triggered a major disruption of the music industry.
- Uber's creation of a new business model that disrupted the taxi industry by providing a more convenient and affordable way to get around in cities.
- Airbnb's creation of a new market for short-term rentals that disrupted the hotel industry by providing a more affordable and personalized experience for travelers.

VERTICAL INNOVATION

This refers to the development of new products, services, or business models that build upon existing offerings or technologies. Vertical innovation can involve improving existing products, entering new markets, or finding new ways to leverage existing capabilities. Examples of vertical innovation include:

- Apple's introduction of the iPhone, which built upon the success of the iPod and added new features and capabilities to create a new market for smartphones.
- Amazon's expansion from an online bookstore to a wide-ranging e-commerce platform that offers a variety of products and services, leveraging its existing capabilities in logistics and customer service.
- Tesla's development of electric vehicles that build upon existing automotive technologies, but offer new features and capabilities such as longer range and autonomous driving.

Both lateral and vertical innovation are important for businesses to remain competitive and meet the evolving needs of customers. Successful companies are able to balance these two approaches to innovation and develop a portfolio of offerings that includes both new and improved products, services, and business models.

In K–12, STEM has been a domain offered as a particular focus for students, classroom and entire schools based on the identified need for technical expertise in Science, Technology, Engineering, and Math.

Schools are expanding their domains providing students with access to high-quality STEM education regardless of their location. For example, online learning resources can be used to provide students with access to STEM courses that are not offered at their school.

The benefits of digital transformation in STEM education are numerous. Students who are able to access technology for STEM subjects are more likely to be engaged and motivated in their studies, they are more likely to develop critical thinking and problem-solving skills, and they are more likely to succeed in STEM-related careers.

ORGANIZATIONAL /CULTURAL TRANSFORMATION

Although digital transformation is focused on improving operations, the impact on the organization, its culture and the individuals cannot be ignored. In fact, the success or failure of any digital transformation initiative might be dependent on the organizational culture and key individuals impacted.

We've just lived through the most fundamental shifts in organizational transformation forced upon us by the COVID-19 pandemic. We know that those schools early to adopt a 1-to-1 computing model were better prepared for online learning than schools experimenting with varying degrees of student device provision. We also know that some students (and teachers) were better prepared for this transition for a variety of reasons.

The short- and long-term impacts of these "last two-years" will be studied and debated for decades. In 2023 we know that the move to online learning was a bumpy one.

Starting with investment in technology resources—infrastructure, Internet services, WIFI, and devices were purchased and distributed with little to no direction of how to achieve their in-person objectives online.

But now that the shift was made, and despite efforts to return to the way it was, we know and recognize many factors of life and learning have changed forever.

Another major factor came through content—web-based services, digital streaming services and the like. Teachers were forced to the lowest common denominator of what services they had and why they just purchased for online learning. But the shift from laptop and teacher-based lesson plans and legacy content was quick to adopt streaming and online services because of the higher production quality.

But the glue that provides the most integration and workflow support is the Learning Management System (LMS). As of today, most schools or districts have tried a few and / or standardized one platform for their schools. Not only does the LMS support video conferencing and messaging for collaboration, they can also manage the homework workflow from syllabus, posting, submission, and review.

These are examples of digital transformation that your school or district has already addressed and survived. This next era of digital transformation will change the workflow and operations of the school and district at its core.

Which begs the question about leadership, strategy and communications.

CHAPTER TWO

CUSTOMER EXPERIENCE TRANSFORMATION

One of the biggest benefits of digital transformation is improved customer experiences. In business, customers expect a seamless and personalized experience when they interact with companies, and digital technologies can enable new methods and modes for the user.

For businesses it's important to understand the customer's perspective with technology. If the customer's expectation is the old way of doing things, do we reject the old way and force them to the new method, or do we transition the customer-base over time?

Obviously, it would be a "what the market will bear" scenario. If customers like and adapt the new model of interaction, then the legacy interface can go away. But if there's a chance some users may want the legacy method, or else, then accommodations must be made for these users. Just think about the chat option that many companies offer on their web pages. Some customers think this manner of communicating with the company is more convenient, while others still want to talk with a real person.

The best option might be to offer both. Another such company may feel that eliminating all people on their help line will ultimately improve their profitability at the cost of customer experience. Again, this becomes a calculated risk.

Many people still look for the ticket window when approaching the cinema or theme park, but we know that we've probably already booked the tickets online and the only reason to stop in front of the entry now is to talk to a person and pay the old way.

An example of an improved customer experience in education is the use of technology to customize the learning experience for particular students. With the help of digital tools, educators can create tailored learning experiences that take into account each student's unique learning style, interests, and abilities.

Adaptive learning platforms use algorithms to analyze student performance and adjust the level and pace of instruction to match their needs. This approach can help students learn more effectively and feel more engaged with the material. Additionally, technology can provide students with greater access to educational resources and support, such as online tutoring, virtual field trips, and digital libraries.

Another example is the use of LMS platforms, which allow students to access resources from anywhere, at any time, and at their own pace. This approach can be particularly beneficial for students who face barriers to attending traditional in-person classes, such as those who live in remote areas, have health issues, or have other responsibilities outside of school.

DIGITAL TRANSFORMATION CHALLENGES & CONCERNS

There are several challenges that organizations face when trying to enhance the customer experience through digital transformation. Some of these include:

Data Privacy and Security

Digital transformation may require an organization to collect and store large amounts of customer data, which may present a significant risk to data privacy and security. Schools must take measures to ensure that student and employee data is properly protected and that Personally Identifiable Information (PII) privacy policies are in place.

As the educational entity begins to analyze and understand how student data can inform the various departments of the school, there must be serious consideration to the understanding of the student and how their personal data might be used and / or made available to others. Who may view what data?

In schools, there is a great divide between student information and student homework data. Although both should be protected, the risk of data privacy breaches of the student personal data is most sensitive and subject to retention policies.

This includes student information systems, and the systems that leverage student data—that's everything from the LMS, Gradebook, Transportation, School Lunch, Pathways, etc. Digital transformation now provides the pathway to access these systems in real-time and provide consolidated reports about these data points.

Integration with Legacy Systems

Many schools still have legacy systems in production that are not easily integrated with new digital technologies. These systems were designed as stand-alone applications and don't provide the application programming interfaces (APIs) to enable other developers to enhance the software.

This can make it difficult to fully leverage newer digital technologies over time and more difficult to improve the customer experience.

Many schools are saddled with Payroll and Finance systems that are run by county or state entities. Each school is limited by the features and use of the system managed by the agency. This makes it difficult to customize the system to accommodate idiosyncrasies of each school or district.

Managing Organizational Change

Digital transformation often requires significant changes to organizational processes and culture. This can be a challenge, as employees may resist change and be resistant to new technologies and processes.

In the example of the phone technicians being displaced by network technicians by VoIP, many of the phone technicians had been around for many years. These were Union jobs where seniority was valued. Many phone technicians considered their jobs unique and irreplaceable.

Most of these technicians were forced into retirement while others had to learn about networks and log into a software PBX system. The cables weren't even the same. Category 6 data communications cable is much different from legacy Category 3 voice cable. The number of twists and total length is quite limited in comparison. The installation process of these data cables is more labor intensive and requires rigid validation testing in order to support multi-gigabit bandwidths. In other words, the transition from legacy technologies was at best, turbulent for some, and at worse, career-ending.

How the organization manages these changes becomes a story of individual success and / or failure for each impacted staff member. Organizational change management in the digital transformation endeavor might be the most important success factor.

Measuring Success

It can be challenging to measure the success of digital transformation efforts, especially when it comes to customer experience. Organizations must develop metrics that accurately reflect the impact of digital transformation on customer experience, and use this data to continuously improve their efforts.

Despite these challenges, organizations that overcome them and effectively leverage digital technologies to enhance the customer experience will be better positioned to compete and succeed in the rapidly changing business environment.

For schools it is more obvious and results driven. Are the students succeeding? Is this demonstrated in their grades and test scores?

TYPES OF DIGITAL TRANSFORMATION AS APPLIED TO K–12 EDUCATION

Digital transformation can have a significant impact on instruction by providing teachers and students with access to a wider range of learning resources, creating personalized learning experiences, improving student engagement, enhancing collaboration, and improving teacher productivity. Digital transformation can help students to learn more effectively and efficiently.

Digital transformation on the operational and administrative side of schools can help to improve efficiency, save money, and improve communication. By embracing digital technologies, schools can make their operations more efficient and effective.

Instructional Process Transformation

This is the same digital transformation described in the author's previous books about Tier 4 Curriculum. Moving your school or district from non-standard, or teacher-selected curriculum, to a district-wide standard, custom developed, Tier 4 Curriculum is a complete digital transformation of how a school district develops, delivers and manages curriculum.

If we're to follow the direction provided in the author's books about T4c, every district should take on the responsibility of developing curriculum with a dedicated team, utilization standards and proliferating an ever expanding library of lesson plans customized for all types of learners and cohorts.

So the focus of this book will be the rest of the organization—Classroom Management, Human Resources, Business Operations, School Administration, Maintenance & Operations, and of course, the Information Technology department.

Curriculum Delivery

Digital transformation can have a significant impact on curriculum delivery in K–12 schools, leading to improvements in the ways that students can learn and ways teachers can teach. Here are some ways that digital transformation can improve curriculum delivery.

INTERACTIVE AND ENGAGING LESSONS

Digital technologies enable teachers to create interactive and engaging lessons that can better hold students' attention and keep them motivated. For example, teachers can use videos, animations, simulations, and other digital resources to explain complex concepts and make learning more interesting and fun.

With a constantly expanding curriculum, and their own ability to adapt the curriculum to each class' and each student's individual needs, each teacher will be able to fine tune their daily lesson plans to the individual needs of the cohort and / or each individual student.

It then becomes contingent for the school to provide learning opportunities, mentoring, coaching and teams to support teachers in the development of customized curriculum.

Tier 4 Curriculum (T4c), as detailed in the author's previous books, provides the strategy for a school or district of any size to begin the move toward development of standardized and customized curriculum.

PERSONALIZED LEARNING

Digital technologies enable teachers to personalize the learning experience for each class and even each student. By customizing lesson plans according to the needs of the individual class, we can see one lesson plan, become two or three lesson plans. Where one history lesson is focused on fundamentals for remedial students, another is focused on standards and grade-level achievement. A third version might be created for advance placement (AP) students utilizing more creative thinking exercises and / or collaboration exercises.

By leveraging data and analytics drawn from the SIS or data integration platform, teachers can gain a deeper understanding of students' strengths, weaknesses, and learning styles, and then tailor lessons and activities to meet their individual needs. This can lead to improved engagement and academic outcomes for students.

ACCESS TO A BROAD RANGE OF DIGITAL AND STREAMING RESOURCES

Digital technologies provide students with access to a vast array of educational resources, including online textbooks, videos, simulations, interactive activities, and immersive simulations. This is a benefit both to the teacher as well as the student. Teachers can draw from this vast array to aid in the communication of lessons within a lesson plan. Students, in the same way, can have access to these resources for research-based projects and synthesis of their own research and homework projects.

Then using the LMS as the glue, teachers can use excerpts, snippets or links to connect the electronic resources into a cohesive, coherent lesson customized for that group of students or individuals.

REAL-TIME FEEDBACK AND ASSESSMENT

Digital technologies can allow for more effective assessment and feedback in the classroom when the features of the LMS are leveraged. Teachers can use LMS-based tools to post homework and detail due dates and other requirements via the calendar and message boards.

Once posted, students can submit completed projects via the LMS, which helps the teacher organize the homework and make them available for digital review.

Once teachers begin the review process, they have the ability to provide students with instant feedback on their submission. This can help teachers identify areas where students need individual help, and can help students understand their own strengths and weaknesses.

But since these interactions can happen in real-time, the old model of completing homework, turning it in, and getting feedback later is gone. This iteration can happen multiple times allowing for multiple revisions and an interactive feedback loop that allows students to zero in to the best submission.

COLLABORATIVE LEARNING

Digital technologies also enable new collaborative learning models, where students can work together on projects and assignments, regardless of their physical location. Once again, the LMS becomes the glue to facilitate these collaborative projects. This leads to improved communication, leadership and teamwork skills, as well as a greater sense of community among students. This is most applicable to how most people collaborate in the workplace today.

In the author's T4c methodology, the 5th and 6th C's are Creative Thinking and Collaboration. These are advanced learning skills enhanced by the LMS and enabling students to learn these skills even if they aren't face-to-face with their peers.

BLENDED LEARNING

Another advanced feature of the LMS enables schools to implement blended learning, which combines traditional classroom instruction with online learning. This provides students with more opportunities to learn at their own pace and in their preferred style, leading to improved academic outcomes.

A group of students might be remote while working with peers in a classroom. These hybrid models are well supported using the LMS to bridge the physical as well as the temporal gap.

Curriculum Development

In the author's previous book *A FAST TRACK TO ONLINE LEARNING: Rapid Development and Deployment of Technology Enabled Curriculum*, the case is made that every school or district MUST develop in-house curriculum development capabilities. The book details how schools can begin to develop curriculum customized to the needs of the students. Designated Tier 4 Curriculum (T4c) and using the 6 C development process, schools can rapidly develop and deploy customized technology enabled curriculum.

Implementing Tier 4 Curriculum and a LMS at your school could, in one initiative, digitally transform the school's whole academic support structure.

Tier 4 Curriculum encompasses the concept of digital everything, synchronous and asynchronous lesson delivery, posting, submission, collaboration, discussion, assessment, cumulation, aggregation and ultimately achievement in testing. T4c empowers the individual teacher to customize and optimize the lesson / curriculum to the needs of the class and even the individual student. Because everything is digital, from content to interaction, all models of remote, hybrid and in-person classes are natively supported.

T4c's model of inherent collaboration allows the teacher to balance group work while enforcing accountability and individual assessment / achievement. How? By requiring aspects of the submission / interaction to be measured and tracked via the LMS.

The integral capability of the LMS system to provide individualized timestamps and history of the student's interaction with the curriculum and their peers within the LMS platform fundamentally renders all activities subject to forensic scrutiny.

AN EXPLOSION OF CURRICULUM GROWTH & CUSTOMIZATION

Once a Tier 4 Curriculum model is adopted, the next stage is an explosion of curriculum growth and customization. Because of the fact that Tier 4 Curriculum is based on standard development and delivery platforms, teachers are empowered to customize the delivery of lesson plans.

New lesson plans can precipitate in horizontal, vertical, and experiential modes. And in multiple ways within these modes.

The approach is designed to be flexible and adaptable, which means that each teacher can modify and add new features to existing lesson plans based on their students' needs and interests. This allows for greater creativity and innovation in the classroom, as well as more personalized learning experiences for each student. By encouraging teachers to contribute to the development of the curriculum, T4c helps to foster a culture of collaboration and continuous improvement in education.

But the alternative model is also the case. If there are no standards for content development and delivery, curriculum will stagnate, and become outdated stores of non-standard curriculum, used by some, and benefitting few. In this scenario, not only is there no incentive for teachers to develop customized curriculum, but there is also no incentive to share, or develop a library of curriculum.

HORIZONTAL EXPANSION MODES

Horizontal expansion of tier 4 curriculum occurs when a lesson plan in one particular subject matter is modified and customized for another subject matter. For instance, a History lesson plan of Old English writer William Shakespeare is modified into a Literature lesson plan of Romeo and Juliet. This mode of curriculum expansion can be modeled across the languages as well as across geographies and cultural studies.

It can easily be demonstrated that a single lesson plan can be the source of several horizontal expansions. Horizontal expansion of T4c could involve applying the approach to different subject areas or grade levels beyond its original scope.

For example, if a T4c lesson plan was initially developed for science classes in high school, a horizontal expansion could involve adapting the approach for use in other subjects such as English or social studies. Another example could be adapting T4c for use in elementary or middle schools, where the focus may be on developing foundational skills or introducing students to a broader range of subjects.

Horizontal expansion could also involve adapting T4c for use in different educational contexts, such as vocational schools, alternative education programs, or distance learning environments. This could help to expand the reach of the approach and make it more accessible to a wider range of students and educators.

The key idea behind horizontal expansion is to take the core principles and strategies of T4c and adapt them to new contexts, subjects, or grade levels, while still maintaining the core focus on personalized and creative learning experiences.

VERTICAL EXPANSION MODES

Vertical expansion modes of curriculum modification is where a lesson plan at one grade-level is modified and customized for another. Moving up and down the discipline, it can easily be seen that a simple grade-level science lesson in cells could become a secondary-level biology, chemistry and even a human biology lesson plan. This type of cross-pollination and elevation of source subject matter, once again, can only come from T4c based on established standards for development and delivery. Seems the author continues to press on the benefits of Tier 4 Curriculum.

Vertical expansion of T4c could involve applying the approach at a larger scale, such as at the school district or state level. This could involve scaling up the approach to reach a larger number of students and educators, and potentially integrating it into broader educational policies and initiatives.

For example, a school district could adopt T4c as its primary approach to curriculum development and teacher training, providing support and resources for teachers to modify and adapt existing lesson plans and collaborate with colleagues. This could lead to greater consistency and standardization in the implementation of T4c across schools and classrooms within the district.

Another example of vertical expansion could involve integrating T4c into broader educational initiatives, such as personalized learning or project-based learning. This could help to align T4c with other educational approaches and goals, and potentially make it more appealing to policymakers and stakeholders at the state or national level.

The key idea behind vertical expansion is to take the core principles and strategies of T4c and apply them at a larger scale, while still maintaining a focus on personalized and creative learning experiences for students.

EXPERIENTIAL EXPANSION MODES

Taking an existing lesson plan, and developing a new lesson plan with a different delivery model is an example of experiential expansion of T4c. Modifying a lecture and practice lesson, into an interactive video and LMS-based submission and peer review practice is an example.

In the author's 6C development process, the fourth C is context. Two contexts are defined, the lesson context and the delivery context. The lesson context is the mode and model the teacher has selected to present the lesson plan, whereas the delivery context is the technology systems and method to deliver the lesson plan.

Updating the lesson context from one scenario to another is an experiential expansion. If the source lesson plan context is to reach a chapter about a king's court, an experiential expansion might be to model the king's court having students taking on the roles of king, advisor, captains and guards.

Experiential expansion of T4c could involve expanding the approach beyond the classroom to include real-world experiences and opportunities for students to engage with the broader community. This could involve incorporating internships, service learning projects, or other forms of experiential learning into the curriculum, in order to give students hands-on experience with the subject matter and help them connect what they are learning to real-world contexts.

For example, a science class using a T4c lesson could incorporate field trips to local environmental sites or labs, allowing students to see and experience the concepts they are learning about in class in a real-world setting. An English class using T4c lessons could incorporate community service projects that involve communication skills, such as writing letters to local representatives or creating content for a community organization's website.

Another example of experiential expansion could involve integrating technology and multimedia into the learning experience, such as creating virtual reality simulations or using online platforms to connect with experts in the field. This could help to create more engaging and interactive learning experiences for students, while still maintaining a focus on personalized and creative learning.

The key idea behind experiential expansion is to expand the learning experience beyond the classroom and provide students with opportunities to apply what they are learning in real-world contexts. By doing so, students can develop a deeper understanding and appreciation for the subject matter, while also gaining valuable skills and experiences that can prepare them for future academic and career opportunities.

Professional Development

One of the most significant areas where digital transformation can impact the organization is Professional Development. If the staff are using curriculum and lesson plans that do not leverage new technologies, their students will likely not benefit either.

Professional development can support digital transformation in instructional processes by helping teachers learn about new technologies, design and deliver engaging and effective digital learning experiences, and create a culture of innovation in their classrooms. By providing teachers with the support they need, professional development plays a critical role in improving student learning outcomes.

Here are some additional tips for creating effective professional development for digital transformation in education:

- Make sure the professional development is relevant to the needs of teachers.
- Provide opportunities for teachers to learn by doing.
- Encourage collaboration and sharing among teachers.
- Make sure the professional development is sustainable and affordable.

DISTRICT OPERATIONAL PROCESS TRANSFORMATION

Departmental Interoperation

Most schools and districts should be somewhere in the process of adopting tools to facilitate automation, integrate communications and workflows, to streamline operations, improve efficiency, and enhance collaboration and communication. That's a mouthful but this is definitely an instance of ESTD—easier said than done. Once again, we're looking for that knight in shining armor to come along and save the day. That person who creates a plan that holds all the answers to automation and information.

One of the key areas where digital transformation can have a significant impact is in the area of departmental interoperations, which refers to the ability of different departments within an organization to work together effectively and efficiently.

In this chapter, we will examine the ways in which digital transformation can be used to enhance departmental interoperability in the school district back office operations. These departments can include any and all of the non-instructional entities that keep schools running including: transportation, food services, maintenance, and operations. All these departments can and should also be benefiting from digital transformation initiatives.

IMPROVED COMMUNICATION AND COLLABORATION

One of the primary ways in which digital transformation can enhance departmental interoperability is by improving communication and collaboration among different departments. Digital technologies, such as online collaboration tools, instant messaging, and video conferencing, allow departments to communicate more easily and effectively with each other, even when they are located in different parts of the building, campus or district. This can greatly enhance the flow of information between departments and reduce the time it takes to complete projects and tasks.

Within most schools and districts, electronic mail has become that ubiquitous communications channel but there are several others that may help, or sometimes hinder, the most efficient and effective types of communications. Yet, as we consider interdepartmental workflows there may be other platforms better suited for interdepartmental communications.

One problem with email is it is asynchronous, meaning people can read and respond to emails at their own convenience, which can lead to delays in communication and collaboration. Although there is the time and date stamp, oftentimes people use their email inbox as a parallel to the old paper-based InBox. First in, first out, and in sequence. Some people who are in the field may wait until the end of each work day to check email, while a chat app might be on their smartphone and allow more responsiveness.

Email is also linear, having initial emails, and their responses, and Reply Alls, creating complex maps of convoluted communications.

Sometimes a chat platform is more real-time and responsive than email. There are a number of other tools that can be more effective for collaboration than email, such as:

Project Management Tools

Although much more complicated than messaging apps, a shared project management document is efficient for providing a shared schedule of projects, resources and timelines. It does require that users have some training and knowledge of project management and GANNT charts, but the benefit definitely outweighs the option of providing status updates via email.

Effective project management tools enable people to track tasks, but also collaborate on documents, and communicate with each other in real time.

Chat Tools

These tools allow people to have instant conversations with each other, which can be helpful for brainstorming and problem-solving. Sometimes you just want to ask someone a quick question—not a formal inquiry. Maybe you're anticipating a quick back-and-forth discussion.

Chat tools are much more effective at this as it's like having a quick verbal conversation. Questions can be asked and answered almost and sometimes faster than a verbal conversation.

There's too many to list but obviously Microsoft and Google have their flavors of chat integrated with their productivity suites. The trick is to find one that everyone likes and understands, and has a license for.

Video Conferencing Tools

These tools allow people to have face-to-face, or live audio conversations, which can be helpful for building relationships and resolving conflicts. Obviously, these require more resources, but almost everyone in business or education today have all the technology resources already. Networking and smart devices and calendar and scheduling software are base-level requirements that almost everyone already is using.

These tools can facilitate any type of interactions today, in fact, software installations and troubleshooting are mostly happening via video conferencing platforms.

INTEGRATED DATA MANAGEMENT

Another key way in which digital transformation can enhance departmental interoperability is through the use of integrated data management systems. These systems allow departments to share data and information in real-time, which can greatly improve the flow of information between departments.

For example, departments can use integrated data management systems to share financial data, customer data, or other key information, which can help to reduce the risk of data duplication, ensure data accuracy, and support better decision-making.

AUTOMATED WORKFLOWS

Digital transformation can also enhance departmental interoperability through the use of automated workflows. Automated workflows allow departments to manage their processes more efficiently and effectively, by reducing the need for manual intervention. For example, departments can use automated workflows to manage approvals, manage project schedules, or allocate resources.

By automating these processes, departments can ensure that they are completed in a timely and accurate manner, which can help to reduce the risk of errors and improve overall departmental performance.

IMPROVED ANALYTICS

Digital transformation can also enhance departmental interoperability by providing departments with improved analytics and reporting capabilities. These capabilities allow departments to monitor their performance and track key metrics, such as project completion rates, resource utilization, and customer satisfaction. By providing departments with this information, digital technologies can help to support better decision-making to improve departmental performance and inform leadership.

Operational Process Transformation

Operational Process Transformation (OPT) within K–12 schools refers to the process of using technology and data to streamline and optimize school operations, with the goal of improving departmental efficiency and maximizing resources. It involves rethinking and redesigning existing processes and systems to improve workflows, reduce costs, and enhance the effectiveness of the school departments.

Some examples of OPT within K–12 schools follow.

AUTOMATING ADMINISTRATIVE TASKS

By using technology to automate tasks such as attendance tracking, grade reporting, and scheduling, valuable time saved can help teachers and administrators focus on more important tasks, such as instruction and student support. The basic tenet that anything that makes the teacher's administrative tasks easier and faster will help to improve the teacher's effectiveness and time spent with student focus.

IMPLEMENTING DATA-DRIVEN DECISION-MAKING

Schools can use data analytics tools to analyze student performance data and identify areas where additional support or intervention is needed. This can help educators make more informed decisions about how to allocate resources and support student success. Also in terms of pathways and career guidance, these beyond curriculum areas can significantly impact the decision-making process for teachers, students and their parents.

ADOPTING AGILE METHODOLOGIES

Agile methodologies, which prioritize flexibility and continuous improvement, can be applied to school operations to allow for rapid iteration and adaptation to changing needs. Agile methodologies include: iterative development, responding to change, self organizing teams and of course, continuous improvement. We'll discuss Agile in more detail in later chapters.

External Business & Operational Systems

Digital transformation can improve external business systems in K–12 schools by leveraging technology to streamline processes, enhance communication, and improve the net efficiency of school operations when dealing with vendors and other external product and service providers. Here are some specific ways in which digital transformation can be applied to improve external business systems in K–12 schools.

ONLINE ENROLLMENT AND REGISTRATION

Digital transformation can help streamline the enrollment and registration process by providing an online platform that allows parents and students to register and submit necessary documentation electronically. This can save time and resources for both schools and families. Most SIS systems provide either web apps or APIs (application programming interfaces) that help automate the enrollment process.

This may be as simple as enabling this feature in your school's current SIS system. Or it can be as complex as having to utilize APIs to pass data between third party online enrollment systems and a legacy SIS system run by another agency, such as a State or County run SIS system.

DIGITAL PAYMENT SYSTEMS

Digital payment systems can be used to streamline the payment process for school fees, lunch fees, and other expenses. This can reduce the administrative burden on school staff and increase transparency for parents and students. The point with this endeavor would be to eliminate the use of cash.

One of the key advantages of digital payment systems is that they can simplify and streamline payment processes, reducing the administrative burden on school staff and enabling more efficient and accurate financial management. No more manual receipts and cash registers.

For example, digital payment systems can enable schools to automate payment processing, reducing the need for manual data entry and minimizing errors and delays. This can help ensure that payments are processed quickly and accurately, reducing the risk of payment disputes or other financial issues.

This is one of those areas where there is likely still a person facilitating manual transaction entries between systems, and unfortunately, the automation of this set of tasks might lead to that person losing their scope of responsibilities.

In addition, digital payment systems can provide greater visibility and transparency into school finances, enabling administrators to track and monitor payments more easily and providing greater insight into revenue and cash flow. This can help schools make more informed financial decisions and improve financial management.

Once again, implementing these advanced capabilities might be easy or difficult based on the systems to be integrated. Again, if these systems are entirely under the purview of your school's leadership, then something can certainly be done.

DATA ANALYTICS

Digital transformation can help schools use data analytics to improve decision-making and identify areas for improvement in school operations. By analyzing data from various operational departments and external sources, schools can gain valuable insights into their operations and make more informed decisions. For example, data analytics can help schools optimize their transportation routes, reducing costs and improving efficiency. It can also be used to identify patterns in deferred maintenance and operational costs, external service fees, and / or subscription services, allowing schools to identify areas where costs can be better contained or even eliminated.

Additionally, data analytics can help schools improve their business systems, such as their financial management and fundraising efforts. By analyzing financial data, schools can identify areas where they may be overspending or where they could cut costs. They can also use data to identify donors who are most likely to give, allowing them to focus their fundraising efforts more effectively.

CLOUD-BASED SYSTEMS

Cloud-based systems can be used to store and share important school data securely and efficiently. This can help schools reduce costs associated with maintaining physical infrastructure and ensure that important data is accessible from anywhere, at any time.

One of the most significant advantages is the ability to access data and applications from any location, as long as there is an internet connection. This means that staff and students can access the resources they need from home or on-the-go, which can improve productivity and flexibility.

Cloud-based systems also offer greater scalability, as schools can easily add or remove resources as their needs change. This can be particularly useful for schools that experience fluctuations in student enrollment or other factors that affect their resource requirements. Additionally, cloud-based systems often offer more robust security measures than traditional on-premises systems, which can help protect sensitive data and ensure compliance with regulations.

Another benefit of cloud-based systems is that they can streamline administrative tasks, such as record-keeping and communication. By automating routine tasks, such as attendance tracking or grade reporting, schools can reduce the administrative burden on staff and free up time for other tasks.

CHAPTER THREE

Masters Concepts in K–12 Digital Transformation

There are several MBA-level concepts that are applicable to digital transformation in K–12 education. Academia has made significant progress in the study of digital transformation in recent years. As technology continues to advance and transform various industries, including education, there has been a growing need for research and scholarship that can help guide and inform the development and implementation of digital transformation initiatives in schools, both from a leadership and administrative perspective, as well as from a teaching and learning perspective.

Higher Education institutions have responded to this need by offering degree programs, courses, and research opportunities that focus specifically on digital transformation in education. These programs often incorporate a multidisciplinary approach, drawing from fields such as education, information technology, business, and psychology, among others. Other sub-categories include: Instructional Technology, Education Technology, Information Technology in Education, Digital Learning and Technology Leadership.

In addition, academic research on digital transformation in education has also evolved over time. There is now a greater focus on understanding the impact of technology on teaching and learning, as well as the factors that contribute to successful digital transformation initiatives in schools. Researchers are also exploring emerging technologies such as artificial intelligence, virtual and augmented reality, and data analytics, and their potential applications in education.

MASTERS SKILLS FOR K–12 DIGITAL TRANSFORMATION

Masters-level skills for K–12 digital transformation are the fundamental skills at the management and leadership level, but aren't necessarily part of an academic degree program. These include: strategic planning, project management, change management, and design thinking. It includes new processes like: Agile, Scrum and Lean management.

These skills are critical for successful digital transformation in schools because they help leaders to effectively plan, manage, and execute digital transformation initiatives, and to ensure that these initiatives are aligned with the needs and goals of all stakeholders, including students, teachers, parents, and administrators.

Additionally, it provides the opportunity to expose teachers and students to the most advanced project management and business leadership methods utilized in the private sector and software development today.

Here are a few examples:

Strategic Planning

Strategic planning is the process of identifying a long-term vision for an organization and then developing a plan to achieve that vision. Strategic planning is a Masters skill that educators must make a personal endeavor to commit to. Why? Because very few educational leaders are asked to develop a strategic plan for digital transformation. But without a strategic plan, there would be no details, no scope or description, no timeline and worst, no real budget or cost estimate.

Strategic planning skills are critical for developing a clear and comprehensive plan, including identifying goals and objectives, assessing risks and opportunities, and developing a roadmap for implementation.

There are many strategic planning methods published and utilized. The author's own method MAPIT® is designed specifically for school districts and technology strategic planning. The important point is that just saying, "we're going to 'digitally transform' our department or district," is meaningless.

A plan that is in someone's head is not a strategic plan. The initiative must be defined and outlined within a strategic plan that lays out scope, budget and timelines. It's important to note that your digital transformation strategic plan will not be called "Digital Transformation Strategic Plan."

It will likely have a name (or should) like "Data Automation Plan" of "Tier 4 Curriculum Plan."

If you need a treatise on MAPIT® Strategic Planning and Project Management, the author has written a whole book on it, called *PROJECT MANAGEMENT IN THE ED TECH ERA: How to Successfully Plan and Manage Your School's Next Innovation,* available where books are sold.

PROJECT MANAGEMENT

Project management is the Masters skill of planning, organizing, and managing resources to achieve a specific goal. Project management skills are essential for overseeing the implementation of complex digital transformation projects, ensuring that they are delivered on time, within budget, and to the required quality standards.

Project Management is the tactical side of strategic planning. Once strategies are in place, then each project plan must be executed. Which means tactical scope, budget and time of the project. Project management is the implementation part of strategic planning and is where the rubber meets the road. Once your strategic plan is accepted, then each individual project will need to be defined, planned and executed.

LEADERSHIP

Leadership is the ability to influence others to coordinate their efforts to achieve a common goal. Leadership is essential for digital transformation in K–12 education because it helps to ensure that the project is advocated and sanctioned from the top-level and the objective is achieved.

In the K–12 education context, leadership is demonstrated not only through spoken word and directive, but also through action. Effective leaders must be able to communicate their vision, goals, and expectations clearly and persuasively, and inspire others to work towards shared objectives. This could not be more relevant than in digital transformation.

Leaders must also lead by example, modeling the behavior and actions they expect of others. This includes demonstrating a commitment to excellence, fostering a culture of continuous learning and improvement, and making difficult decisions when necessary to achieve organizational goals. And not forwarding that inappropriate email joke video.

COMMUNICATION

Communication is the process of exchanging information. Passing relevant data between parties working toward a common goal.

Communication is essential for digital transformation in K–12 education because it helps to ensure that everyone is on the same page and that there is a shared understanding of the challenges and opportunities facing the school or district.

Communication is also the key to successful project management as well as successful problem management and change management. If there is a problem, and your team is proactively communicating potential down times and resolutions, then the problem becomes an irritant.

If the problem and its resolution are not successfully communicated, then the whole down time has been a tragic failure of operations and communication. In the context of digital transformation in schools, communication of intent, plans, and impacts will be the key to success and failure.

In essence, a project could fail, yet good communication can mitigate disaster, while also the opposite is true.

AGILE METHODOLOGY

Agile methodology is an approach to project management that emphasizes flexibility and collaboration. This approach can be particularly useful in the context of digital transformation in K–12 education, where technology and educational needs are rapidly evolving.

By emphasizing quick and continuous delivery of working software and technology solutions, agile management can help institutions rapidly prototype and iterate new solutions, adapting to changing requirements and market demands as they arise. Additionally, collaborative planning and decision-making can help organizations align their digital transformation efforts with the needs of students, faculty, and staff.

Flexibility and adaptability inherent in agile management can help institutions navigate the complex and rapidly evolving process of digital transformation. Fundamentally, agile management's focus on iteration and continuous improvement focuses organizations to refine and improve their technology solutions over time, ensuring that they remain relevant and effective in the face of ongoing changes in technology and the educational landscape.

DESIGN THINKING

Design thinking is a problem-solving approach that emphasizes empathy, experimentation, and iteration. This approach can be useful in designing and developing lesson plans that meet the specific needs of students, teachers, and other stakeholders in K–12 education.

This methodology emphasizes a human-centered approach to problem-solving, focusing on understanding and empathizing with the needs and perspectives of users. This approach is particularly relevant to the context of digital transformation in schools, as technology solutions need to be designed according to the needs of the teachers, their subject matter and their pedagogy, relative to their students and understanding and being responsive to their specific learning needs.

By placing users at the center of the design process, design thinking can help schools create subject matter and lesson plans that are effective, relevant, and well-suited to the needs of the students and the educational institution holistically.

Design thinking also encourages an iterative approach to prototyping and testing new teaching methods and lesson plan approaches. This allows schools to rapidly experiment with different means and methods and refine them based on student feedback and outcomes. This is a key success tenet of Tier 4 Curriculum.

BUSINESS PROCESS REENGINEERING

Business process reengineering is a method for improving organizational performance by redesigning key business processes. This is just another definition of digital transformation when the reengineering leverages technology for the recognition of efficiency and effectiveness. Business process reengineering (BPR) can be an effective approach for educational institutions seeking to undergo digital transformation.

This is a more structured and business oriented approach that can be useful in identifying opportunities for digital transformation on the administrative and operations of K–12 education, such as streamlining administrative tasks or automating curriculum development practices.

BPR involves analyzing existing business processes with the aim of identifying opportunities for improvement, and then redesigning these processes to improve efficiency, effectiveness, and customer satisfaction. In the context of digital transformation in education, BPR can be applied in several ways.

This could involve, for example, analyzing the process of course delivery and identifying ways in which technology solutions such as online learning platforms or virtual classrooms could be integrated to make the process more efficient and effective. This could involve redesigning the process for student assessment, for example, to make use of automated grading systems or adaptive assessment tools.

BPR can involve integrating technology solutions into business processes to optimize performance. This could involve integrating technology solutions using application programming interfaces (APIs) that allow customization of standard platforms, such as learning management systems, student information systems, or integrating data analytics into existing administrative processes, to make these systems more integrated and eliminating manual operations.

VUCA ASSESSMENT

VUCA (Volatility, Uncertainty, Complexity, Ambiguity) assessment is highly relevant to schools undergoing digital transformation. The VUCA concept is used to describe the rapidly changing and unpredictable nature of the modern educational landscape. This includes factors such as technological advancements, shifting demographics, and changes in the socio-economic environment.

Today, following the COVID era, teachers, administrators, and students are faced with complex challenges that require them to be flexible, adaptable, and able to navigate uncertainty. Digital transformation involves significant changes to how education is delivered, managed, and supported, and can be a complex and uncertain process. VUCA provides a useful framework for understanding and managing the challenges and opportunities of digital transformation.

Volatility refers to the speed and unpredictability of change, which is a common symptom of digital transformation in schools. The salient point is that when planning for digital transformation, or more specifically, when planning to implement a new delivery method or lesson plan delivery context, it is valuable to understand the impact on students and teachers subject to this change.

What are the potential side-effects of this volatility? Are the students ready for this change? How can we prepare them better?

Uncertainty relates to the lack of predictability and the inability to foresee future events and outcomes. Under the heading of volatility, we asked about side-effects. The reality is that we can't foresee all the side-effects. What do we do when students are suddenly presented with new platforms that they are unfamiliar with? Can we mitigate these side-effects with communication and training?

Complexity refers to the intricate nature of digital transformation and the technology systems adopted for the teaching methodology, which often involves multiple interrelated factors and stakeholders. Think of the layers of technology, infrastructure, devices and platforms that form the basis of these new teaching methods.

An understanding of the fundamentals for all these is requisite to success in this new age. The VUCA assessment becomes the inquiry that can expose these risks and allow those in the planning to anticipate and mitigate these risks.

Ambiguity refers to the lack of clarity or understanding about the implications and consequences of digital transformation. Once again, we're trying to understand the nascent and underlying impacts that may be hidden under the plans for a new paradigm of digital transformation.

There are a number of key factors that can be used to assess if VUCA is impacting a school or district. Although some of them are not in the technology or digital transformation realm, they warrant similar considerations. These factors include:

- The pace of change: Is the school or district struggling to keep up with the pace of change? Are there new technologies, educational trends, or societal changes that the school or district is not prepared for?
- The level of uncertainty: Is the future of the school or district uncertain? Are there economic, political, or social factors that could impact the school or district in the future?
- The level of complexity: Is the school or district facing a complex set of challenges? Are there multiple factors that are impacting the school or district, and are these factors interrelated?
- The level of ambiguity: Are there situations where there is no clear right or wrong answer? Are there challenges that the school or district is facing that are difficult to define or understand?

The VUCA framework can be applied to schools and school districts as they face complex and uncertain futures. The VUCA mindset can help school administrators, teachers, and staff to navigate the challenges and uncertainties they face in their day-to-day work and help communicate and prepare staff, teachers, students, and parents for these potential risks and unknowns.

For example, schools and school districts may face VUCA challenges such as changes in student demographics, declining enrollment, budget cuts, technological advancements, and leadership changes. By understanding the VUCA framework, educators and school leaders can develop strategies to address these challenges, such as building resilience, developing adaptive leadership skills, and promoting collaboration and creativity.

VUCA AND CRISIS PREPARATION AND RESPONSE

Moreover, VUCA assessment can help schools and school districts to prepare for and respond to unexpected crises such as natural disasters, school shootings, and pandemics. In years past, we could ignore such scenarios, but today, we must have both preparation and technology systems that can help mitigate these scenarios.

By anticipating potential VUCA scenarios and developing contingency plans, school leaders can ensure that their schools are better equipped to manage crises and provide a safe and supportive learning environment for students and staff. There are several indicators that can help determine if schools or school districts are being impacted by VUCA. Here are a few examples:

Rapid Changes in Student Demographics

Changes in student demographics can create VUCA challenges for schools and school districts, such as language barriers, cultural differences, and varying educational needs. If a school or district is experiencing rapid changes in student demographics, this may be an indicator of VUCA.

A rapid influx of migrants from other countries is a known and topical VUCA phenomenon. Not only does it trigger a vast change in the student demographic, but the economic impact is also directly affected.

These students have very little exposure to the technology systems our students take for granted. Will these students be able to assimilate and utilize the advanced platforms or must the school provide low-level training in the fundamental skills required to become part of the educational community they have become part of?

Technological Advancements

Advances in technology are changing the way students learn and interact with the world. Schools and districts that are struggling to keep up with these changes may be experiencing VUCA challenges.

If schools are able to provide the fundamental technologies to students: network infrastructure (WIFI and Internet), devices and core LMS systems, they have the necessary technology to respond to VUCA technological challenges.

But the technology does not do this automatically, the plans must be written, the training performed, and the changes executed. School districts must have actively monitored help desk environments, and technically capable IT engineering staff, first to support and manage the infrastructure, and second, to be able to assess, plan, adapt as necessary in response to VUCA.

Budget Cuts and Policy Changes

Budget cuts and changes in education policy can create uncertainty and instability for schools and districts, making it difficult to plan and implement effective strategies.

By embracing the VUCA mindset, school districts can develop a posture of flexibility, adaptability, and resilience. This means being willing to consider new approaches and ideas, being open to feedback and input from stakeholders, and being willing to make difficult decisions when necessary.

If a school district is faced with budget cuts, they may need to consider new cost-saving measures, such as reducing staff or cutting back on certain programs. By approaching the situation with a VUCA mindset, district leaders can work collaboratively with stakeholders to identify areas where cuts can be made while minimizing the impact on student learning.

Natural Disasters or Other Crises

Schools and districts that have experienced natural disasters or other crises may be dealing with VUCA challenges as they work to respond and recover. Implementing VUCA fundamentals would prepare leadership with contingency plans for such a crisis.

Low Student Achievement

Schools and districts that are struggling to improve student achievement despite their efforts may be facing VUCA challenges. This may be an indicator of a need to adapt to new teaching and learning methods or to address underlying issues related to student learning and development.

A VUCA response might include early intervention plans, student progress tracking, differentiation of instruction for at-risk student groups and collaboration to enhance engagement.

MASTERS PROGRAMS IN K–12 DIGITAL TRANSFORMATION

Both MBA and Masters of Arts in Education programs have recognized the need for understanding and mastering the concepts of digital transformation in schools. MBA programs have long emphasized the importance of technology in business operations and have recognized the potential of technology to improve organizational efficiency and effectiveness.

In recent years, Masters programs have increasingly focused on the role of technology in education and the need for school leaders to develop digital literacy and technology management skills. Both corporate education and professional development programs as well as traditional K–12 education are similarly studied in today's MA Ed. programs.

Masters of Arts in Education programs have recognized the impact of advanced technology to improve teaching and learning outcomes well beyond the fundamentals for wireless devices, classroom technology and networking. Most universities offer focus or special certification in Instructional and Educational Technology.

Here are some examples:

Master of Science in Learning Design and Technology: This program focuses on the intersection of instructional design, educational psychology, and technology. Students in this program learn how to develop effective and engaging digital learning experiences.

Master of Science in Educational Technology: This program focuses on the integration of technology in K–12 education. Students in this program learn how to design and implement technology-rich learning environments and how to evaluate the effectiveness of technology integration.

Master of Education in Digital Learning and Leading: This program focuses on the role of technology in transforming teaching and learning. Students in this program learn how to use technology to promote innovation, creativity, and collaboration in the classroom.

Master of Arts in Educational Media: This program focuses on the development and production of digital media for educational purposes. Students in this program learn how to design and produce digital media that supports teaching and learning outcomes.

Doctor of Education in Educational Technology Leadership: This program focuses on the leadership skills needed to implement effective technology integration in K–12 education. Students in this program learn how to develop and implement technology plans, evaluate technology integration, and promote digital citizenship.

ADVANCED TECHNOLOGIES IN K–12 DIGITAL TRANSFORMATION

K–12 schools have already moved way past fundamental technologies such as devices, networks and interactive white boards, and have moved on to advanced technology platforms and systems. Advanced technologies leverage existing infrastructure and least common denominator systems to provide advanced technology capabilities that go way beyond the fundamentals.

With the increasing demand for digital literacy and the need for students to be prepared for a digital world, K–12 schools have transitioned the focus beyond LMS and student devices to integrated technology systems such as virtual and augmented reality, gamification, learning analytics, robotics, coding, and artificial intelligence.

These advanced technologies help provide a more engaging and personalized learning experience, enabling students to explore complex concepts in a multi-input, multi-dimensional way.

Virtual and Augmented Reality (VR/AR)

VR and AR technologies are being introduced as a means of creating immersive learning experiences. These technologies can be used to simulate real-world scenarios, provide virtual field trips, and enable students to explore complex concepts in a visually engaging way. Using computer-based simulations, or full-scale virtual reality goggles, that provide a 360° interactive world that users can move around and interact with.

Although these immersive experiences still don't allow for walking and actually touching the simulated world, what can be accomplished with just VR goggles is immersive enough to make some users motion sick and other experiential feelings.

Unfortunately, these immersive systems are not complete and foolproof, they are still simulations and require sophisticated compute and interactive components not available to most end-users. These examples are also limited in the respect that they are so specific to a subject matter, that the simulation might only be applicable to one or a few lesson plans.

Additionally, these immersive systems do not lend themselves to the classroom model, where 1 teacher and 30 students must spend 50 minutes of learning time per period. Systems like these become options for leveraged learning opportunities or customized pathways.

Gamification

Gamification is the use of game design elements in learning or lesson plan contexts as a way of increasing student engagement and motivation. Gamification can be used to create interactive learning experiences, provide instant feedback, and incentivize student participation.

Gamification increases student engagement because the interaction provides the look, feel and sense of engagement as video games and competitions.

Once again however, these gamified lesson plans must be authored and developed by someone or some company. And these solutions are out there but not proliferating as quickly as would be required to become a phenomenon of its own. Additionally, these third party games and simulations might not adhere to the lesson plan guidelines as defined for your school.

In a T4c scenario, an initial lesson plan developed under the standards of districts embracing T4c, teachers would be able to modify the lesson plan and make more vertical, horizontal and experientially expanded lessons.

Learning Analytics

Learning analytics is the use of data analysis techniques to improve teaching and learning outcomes. Advanced technologies are introducing systems using learning analytics as a way of identifying student needs, tracking student progress, and assessing the effectiveness of instructional practices.

Descriptive Analytics

This type of analytics involves collecting and analyzing data to describe what has happened in the past. It provides insights into student performance, behavior, and engagement. Using this data, lessons can be adapted and customized to focus on a student's strengths and weaknesses. Once again however, unless developed under a T4c scenario, teachers may not have the tools or training to customize and continue development of these lesson plans.

Diagnostic Analytics

Diagnostic analytics is used to identify the root cause of a problem. This type of analytics involves analyzing data to understand why a particular problem has occurred. As related to lesson plans and testing, results are analyzed and the data bear out areas of the student's strengths and weaknesses. As an example of personalized learning, there must be a reality check as to whether teachers have the bandwidth and aptitude to customize or adapt lesson plans to individual students based on need.

Predictive Analytics

Predictive analytics is used to forecast what might happen in the future. It uses historical data to make predictions about future student performance or behavior. Although it might seem that historical data is just that—history, it can be used to identify students at risk of difficulties or failure. It's clear that it becomes contingent upon the teacher to review the analytics and make these curricular adjustments. The point is, that data is there.

Prescriptive Analytics

Prescriptive analytics provides recommendations on what actions to take based on the data collected. It involves analyzing data to provide actionable insights that can improve student outcomes.

For instance, prescriptive analytics might recommend that a particular student receive additional

one-on-one support from a teacher or participate in an after-school tutoring program. The prescriptive analytics might also recommend modifications to the student's learning plan, such as offering different types of learning materials or providing more challenging assignments.

Natural Language Processing

Natural Language Processing (NLP) involves analyzing written or spoken language to identify patterns or trends. It can be used to analyze student writing or speech to provide feedback on their performance or to identify areas for improvement.

These different types of learning analytics can be used to help educators make data-driven decisions that improve student outcomes, enhance the teaching and learning experience, reinforce student pathway opportunities and support the overall goals of the educational institution.

CODING

Coding is a key component of digital transformation at several levels. Fundamentally, offering coding classes in K–12 grades is the best way to prepare students for the digital age and careers working in software development and core technology trades and professions. Experience in coding empowers students with the understanding of creating software apps that impact theirs and the lives of their application users.

These are the most common areas introduced and relevant in coding.

Scratch

Scratch is a visual programming language developed by MIT that allows students to create interactive stories, animations, and games using drag-and-drop blocks of code. It's designed to be easy to use, making it a popular choice for elementary and middle school students.

Python

Python is a popular general-purpose programming language that's widely used in industry and academia. It's often taught in high school computer science courses as an introduction to text-based programming. Python's syntax is designed to be easy to read and understand, making it a good choice for beginners.

Java

Java is a widely-used programming language that's often taught in advanced high school computer science courses. Java's syntax is more complex than Python, but it's also more powerful and versatile. Java is used extensively in industry for developing enterprise applications, mobile apps, and video games.

HTML/CSS

HTML and CSS are markup languages used to create websites. They are often taught in K–12 schools as an introduction to web development. Students learn how to create and style web pages using HTML and CSS, which are essential skills for careers in web design and development.

App Inventor

App Inventor is a visual programming environment developed by MIT that allows students to create mobile apps for Android devices using drag-and-drop blocks of code. It's designed to be easy to use, making it a popular choice for middle and high school students interested in mobile app development.

Robotics

Robotics is the physical extension of coding. The ability to manipulate nature and physics using a combination of computers, programming, electronics and machinery. It is the ultimate expression of digital transformation. Think of the crane, the tractor, and the surgical robot.

Robotics technologies are being studied in K–12 programs as a means of developing students' computational thinking skills and preparing them for careers in the digital economy. These technologies can be used to teach physics, mechanics, problem-solving, critical thinking, and collaboration skills.

Following are the most predominant types of robotics relevant today.

Educational Robotics

Educational robotics is designed to teach students about the principles of robotics and engineering. These robots are simple to build and program, and they can be used to teach students about concepts such as mechanics, motion, sensors, and actuators. They are typically kits that can be programmed for specific types of robotic operations, such as:

- Line follower robots: These robots are designed to follow a line on the ground. They are often used in educational robotics programs to teach students about basic programming concepts. These might include sensors, lights, motors, servos and actuators.
- Obstacle avoidance robots: These robots are designed to avoid obstacles in their path. They are often used in educational robotics programs to teach students about sensors and navigation.
- Puzzle-solving robots: These robots are designed to solve puzzles. They are often used in educational robotics programs to teach students about problem-solving and logic. These tend to focus less on physical challenges although these can easily include motors and actuators.
- Competition robots: These robots are designed to compete in robotics competitions. They are often more complex and challenging to build and program than educational robots. There robots might be programmed to push each other out of a ring, solve mazes or play soccer.

- Research robots: These robots are designed to conduct research. They are often used to solve real-world problems, such as exploring space, detecting landmines, and assisting the elderly.

Competition Robotics

Competition robotics is a great way for students to apply the skills they learn in educational robotics. These robots are typically more complex and challenging to build and program, and they are often used to compete in events such as FIRST LEGO League, VEX Robotics Competition, BEST Robotics Competition and the RoboCup Junior competition.

GOVERNANCE, DISTRICT POLICY AND DIGITAL TRANSFORMATION

We know not how hard it is to implement a technology initiative until a spark causes a fire and the issue rises to the level of the school board. As the saying goes, the road to hell is paved with good intentions. Digital transformation is always intended to be a positive endeavor, but until someone or some interest group is injured, then the school board gets involved, and then all bets are off.

Several examples of new technologies that had been banned include cell phones, social media (remember MySpace) and some educational apps that could be used to enable cheating or accessing inappropriate content.

Banning these technologies was always a knee-jerk reaction until new policies and guidelines could be established to manage and monitor how these technologies could be allowed. With some of these examples, we've cringed, weathered the storm, and accepted that there are platforms and technologies that offer more benefit, than when banning them trying to mitigate bad behavior.

Once again acceptable use, modeling behavior and training are the success factors.

Digital transformation in K–12 education raises several policy issues for school boards. Here are a few examples.

Governance & Digital Transformation

Governance is essential for the successful implementation of digital transformation in K–12 education. It may involve policy development, resource allocation, curriculum development, risk management, and collaboration among different stakeholders.

Policies should be defined and adopted to govern the use of technology in K–12 education, protecting student privacy and defining how technology can support teaching and learning, as well as how technology systems should be leveraged to benefit school operations and administration.

Governance can help guide digital literacy and technology-based curriculum development ensuring that students have the necessary skills to benefit from the use of technology effectively. These guidelines would umbrella the district's T4c development processes and procedures.

Risk management is important to manage cybersecurity risks, protect student data, and ensure that technology is used in a safe and responsible manner. One key aspect of resource allocation in risk management is ensuring that there is adequate funding and staffing to support digital transformation initiatives.

This may include investments in hardware and software, as well as ongoing support and maintenance costs. Schools must also ensure that there are sufficient human resources available to manage the implementation and ongoing operation of digital technologies, including IT staff and technology coaches.

Large school districts should have a dedicated Risk Manager but smaller districts typically don't have an FTE dedicated risk manager position. In some cases, the responsibilities of risk management may be divided among different staff members or departments, such as the business office, safety or security office, or legal department.

Another important aspect is the allocation of resources to address potential risks and challenges that may arise during the implementation of digital transformation initiatives. This may include allocating funds to address cybersecurity risks, investing in training and professional development for staff, or establishing contingency plans for potential disruptions to technology infrastructure. All things that have been mentioned before, but not under the lens of governance.

Governance can help facilitate collaboration and coordination among different stakeholders to ensure that everyone is working towards the same goals and that technology is used effectively to support teaching and learning. In the context of digital transformation, governance is important for ensuring that the transformation is aligned with the organization's strategic goals and that it is implemented in a way that minimizes risk. Collaboration is important for ensuring that the transformation is successful.

There are a number of ways in which governance can be used to promote collaboration among stakeholders in digital transformation. One way is to create a governance structure that includes representatives from all of the key departmentals stakeholders. This will help to ensure that everyone has a voice in the decision-making process and that the transformation is aligned with the needs of all stakeholders.

Another way to promote collaboration is to establish clear roles and responsibilities for each stakeholder. This will help to ensure that everyone knows what they are responsible for and that there is no overlap or confusion.

Most importantly, it is critical to create a culture of trust and cooperation among stakeholders. This will help to ensure that everyone is willing to share information and work together to achieve the common goal of successful digital transformation.

To support this, the school district creates a digital transformation committee that includes stakeholders from the school board, administration, teachers, parents, and students. The committee is responsible for developing policies and procedures that govern the use of technology in education and ensuring that all are involved in the decision-making process.

The committee develops policies and procedures that address key areas such as data privacy, cybersecurity, and acceptable use of technology. These recommendations become part of the AUP. These policies and procedures are communicated to all stakeholders, and training is provided to ensure that everyone understands their responsibilities.

The school district allocates resources to support digital transformation initiatives, such as upgrading the school's Wi-Fi network, providing devices to students, and training teachers and staff.

Equity and Access to District-based resources

School boards must adopt policies and identify funding sources that support programs to ensure all students have access to the technology and digital resources, as well as the connectivity and access to curriculum and streaming services necessary to participate along with all their peers.

We've talked about it earlier in passing, but one of the most pressing policy issues related to digital transformation is ensuring equity and access to technology for all students. And that's not just a device and some electronic resources.

Without Internet connectivity, these devices are mostly useless. So not only the initial capital investment drives the devices and infrastructure, but operational costs and subscriptions services are also considerations for public WIFI and HotSpots.

Privacy and Security of District Data and Infrastructure

Digital transformation also raises risks around student data privacy and cybersecurity. School boards must adopt policies and fund services that protect student data privacy and ensure that digital resources are secure and not vulnerable to cyber threats. We'll be taking a deeper dive into Cybersecurity risks for individuals as well as the school itself in later chapters.

District IT services must be proactive in Cybersecurity policies and services. Whether on-prem or in the cloud, implementing subscription-based services to ensure service levels for these types of risks should be part of an operational budget.

Digital Citizenship and the AUP

Digital transformation requires students as well as teachers and staff to develop digital citizenship skills, including responsible and ethical use of technology. Teaching, demonstrating and enforcing digital citizenship is a critical aspect of digital transformation and will become an underlying cultural factor in your school.

Just as in the community, the mores of general behavior are based on the leadership and enforcement of the community. If either of these are lacking, then the rest of the community will join in with the behavior.

The best way for schools to teach and enforce digital citizenship is through a comprehensive approach that includes both education and an Acceptable Use Policy (AUP).

The AUP is a board approved policy document that provides the guidelines and enforcement protocols in support of digital citizenship in schools. The AUP outlines the acceptable uses of technology and digital resources in schools, as well as the consequences for inappropriate use.

The AUP helps to enforce digital citizenship by providing clear guidelines for responsible and ethical use of technology. It sets expectations for appropriate behavior, such as not engaging in cyberbullying or harassment, not accessing inappropriate content, and not using technology for illegal activities. By enforcing these expectations, the AUP helps to create a safe and positive online environment for students and staff.

It is an important tool for ensuring that BOTH students and staff are aware of their responsibilities when using technology and digital resources. Teachers must be aware of their role in teaching, demonstrating, and policing of the policies.

Schools should provide digital citizenship education that is integrated into the curriculum and emphasizes responsible and ethical use of technology. This technology fundamental should begin at an early age and continue throughout a student's K–12 career. It should cover topics such as online safety, privacy, cyberbullying, and digital footprint. These training and practices must be enforced and revisited frequently with the Acceptable Use Policy (AUP).

Fundamentals of Digital Tools—Teacher Training

Schools and districts need to provide teachers with the fundamental training they need to use digital learning tools effectively. Each district should ensure that every teacher understands how their suite of classroom and teaching tools works and the way the district Instructional Services advocates and supports.

Whether supported through district instructional resources, coaches and / or mentoring programs. Teachers should have guidelines and standards for how they utilize technology tools and train their students. These should be primarily focused on the LMS and all its available tools, and the productivity suite of choice.

This training should cover topics such as how to use digital tools to differentiate instruction, how to assess student learning, and how to manage student behavior in online learning environments. Schools and districts can provide this training through professional development workshops, online courses, and other resources.

The funding for these rigors should be part of an annual operational training budget, not as a one-and-done, off-year anomaly.

Differentiate Instruction

Differentiating instruction is the practice of tailoring teaching methods and materials to meet the individual needs of students. A suite of classroom tools can be used to help teachers differentiate instruction effectively. For example, technology tools such as online learning platforms, interactive whiteboards, and educational apps can provide students with opportunities to engage with material at their own pace and in their own way.

When practiced in a T4c environment, one or two simple modifications or changes in lesson or delivery context can differentiate the lesson. The focus is to make each learning opportunity engaging and unique. Think about affecting vertical, horizontal and / or experiential differentiation and enhancement of existing lesson plans.

Teachers can also use the LMS assessment tools to gather data on student performance and use this information to personalize and focus instruction.

Classroom Management

Classroom management tools such as seating charts, wireless automated attendance, and behavior tracking systems can help teachers create a positive and supportive learning environment that fosters student success. By using a suite of classroom tools, teachers can differentiate instruction in a way that supports student learning and promotes academic growth.

Once again, the LMS should become the centerpoint of classroom management. By leveraging all the services and features of the LMS and its integration with the SIS, this will become the base-level standard that all students and teachers are familiar with. Even if other software or services are available, by standardizing on the LMS-based features, this ensures everyone understands the feature-set of the default suite.

Some classroom management features might be part of your student information system since these tie directly back to the classroom / teacher assignments, etc., but since most LMS systems also integrate with SIS systems, these features should be available via the LMS.

Accountability to the Plan

After the evaluation stage, there must be accountability. Not to fix blame but to continue on the improvement cycle. Schools and districts need to identify the metrics they will adopt to measure the impact of digital transformation on student learning.

Gather relevant data throughout the digital transformation process. This can include student performance data, engagement metrics, attendance rates, discipline records, teacher feedback, and other relevant data points. These are data points already being tracked and reported but they likely aren't analyzed in the context of digital transformation initiatives.

Classroom engagement and student behavior statistics also inform the teacher but these may require APIs and teacher observation and assessment to facilitate data collection.

Analyze this data to identify trends, patterns, and improvements resulting from the initiatives.

Data-driven insights can help showcase the positive impact of digital transformation on various aspects of education.

Once digital transformation initiatives are kicked-off, set a baseline for key metrics such as ELA, Mathematics, and Graduation Rates. Schools and districts can also use surveys and interviews to collect feedback from students, teachers, and parents about the impact of digital transformation.

TECHNOLOGY SYSTEMS LIFECYCLE INFRASTRUCTURE AND SUPPORT

Digital transformation also requires schools to have the necessary infrastructure and support systems in place to support technology integration. These systems are not static. Not only are they dynamic but they are practically disposable. Especially when it comes to student and teacher devices.

Unlike school buildings and stadiums which have a life cycle of 50 to 80 years, technology systems max out at 7 years, devices 5 years, and technology infrastructure 15 years. But by understanding these lifecycles for technology systems, district strategic planning for IT systems and support will be better served.

Effective management of the technology system lifecycle is important for several reasons. It helps schools to ensure that they are making strategic investments in technology that align with their educational goals and priorities. By carefully planning and evaluating technology investments at each stage of the lifecycle, schools can avoid investing in technology that does not meet their needs or support their educational objectives.

Second, effective management of the technology system lifecycle helps schools to ensure that their technology infrastructure is reliable and secure. This includes ongoing maintenance contracts and upgrades to hardware and software, as well as regular monitoring and testing of technology systems to identify and address potential security risks or vulnerabilities.

Effective management of the technology system lifecycle helps schools to control costs and manage resources more effectively. By carefully planning and budgeting for technology investments at each stage of the lifecycle, schools can avoid unexpected expenses and ensure that they are investing resources in a sustainable way that supports their long-term goals and objectives.

School boards must develop policies and standards for technology lifecycle and support that ensure that schools have the necessary infrastructure, technical support, and resources needed to effectively integrate technology into teaching and learning for perpetuity.

CHAPTER FOUR

Cybersecurity Issues in Education

Of course, we can't have a discussion about digital transformation without the obligatory cybersecurity discussion. It seems like Moore's law also applies to cybersecurity, "the number of viruses, malware, hacks and digital afflictions doubles every eighteen months." New and more destructive forms of viruses continue to proliferate even faster and with equal devastation as COVID-19.

If your school district IT services are not effectively training and managing the current round of Cybersecurity threats in your organization, then your school district may well not flourish through digital transformation, but may also be strangled and / or held hostage by its malevolent sub-entities.

Here's a recent list of some computer viruses that have been specifically targeted at schools or educational institutions.

> SchoolSafe—a ransomware that specifically targets educational institutions and demands payment to unlock the encrypted data, such as confidential student data or payroll data.
>
> Mirai—a malware that targets IoT devices, including those used in schools, and can be used for DDoS attacks. These attacks affect the performance of a school's entire network and Internet access.
>
> Locky—a ransomware that has been known to target educational institutions and infects systems through phishing emails.
>
> Gamarue—a botnet malware that has been known to target educational institutions and can be used for spamming and DDoS attacks.

Stay tuned next week for a completely new and more dangerous list.

COMMON CYBERSECURITY RISKS

Schools need to be ahead of the curve regarding cybersecurity risks because they hold sensitive and confidential information about students, faculty, and staff, including personal and financial data. This information is attractive to cybercriminals who can use it for identity theft, financial fraud, or other criminal activities. In addition, schools are increasingly using technology to deliver educational services and manage administrative tasks, which means that they are vulnerable to a wide range of cyber threats, such as ransomware attacks, phishing scams, and data breaches.

Being ahead of the curve in terms of cybersecurity means that schools are proactive in identifying and addressing potential cyber threats, rather than waiting for an incident to occur. This involves implementing a robust cybersecurity strategy that includes regular risk assessments, security audits, and staff training on best practices for cybersecurity. It also involves investing in cybersecurity technologies such as firewalls, antivirus software, and intrusion detection systems, and regularly updating them to stay current with emerging threats.

Here are the most common cybersecurity risks most schools should be aware of and train their users about.

Phishing and Social Engineering

Malicious attacks can affect any business or individual and can just as easily impact a school or entire district. Everything from the basic advertising virus to ransomware is introduced into organizations via Phishing or Social Engineering—mostly via email.

Since practically all school districts are providing student emails, they've become an easy target for attacks. So along with the first email account provided by the school, should be basic Cybersecurity training, and acceptable use policies. Students must be made aware of how their individual Internet interactions can and will threaten each of their peers, and the school as a whole.

Once again, the district's IT department must have a license to the latest and greatest in email filters and scanning software. Once again, don't even consider not using SaaS (Software as a Service) for these types of applications. Not only are you ensuring your institution's solution is up-to-date, but moving to cloud-based services is a digital transformation in-and-of-itself.

Phishing attacks are where cybercriminals use deceptive emails, texts, or social media messages to trick school staff into providing sensitive information, such as login credentials to their secure services.

A school's students and staff can easily be targeted because of their mail formats and special interest in scholarships, financial aid and fundraising.

These may look like innocent emails from your own organization that trick you into clicking on buttons and resetting or providing old passwords.

Following are the most common phishing and social engineering attacks:

Fake Login Pages

In this type of phishing attack, attackers create a fake login page that looks identical to the legitimate login page of a school's learning management system or email system. The attackers then send a phishing email to students or staff members, urging them to click on a link and log in to their account. When the users enter their login credentials, the attackers capture their username and password, giving them access to sensitive data.

Gift Card Scams

In this type of phishing attack, attackers send phishing emails to school staff members, posing as senior administrators, asking them to purchase gift cards and provide the card details. The attackers then use these cards for fraudulent activities. Be sure you're well aware of the school's sanctioned fundraising opportunities and report any other emails to IT.

Financial Aid Scams

In this type of phishing attack, attackers send phishing emails to students, posing as financial aid offices, asking them to provide sensitive information, such as social security numbers, to process their financial aid application. High Juniors and Seniors are particular targets for these scams.

COVID-19 Scams

With the COVID-19 pandemic, attackers have been using phishing emails that impersonate health organizations or school officials, requesting sensitive information, such as health data or login credentials, under the guise of helping to prevent the spread of COVID-19.

Job Offer Scams

In this type of phishing attack, attackers create fake job offers to lure students or staff members into sharing their personal information, such as social security numbers, bank account details, and other sensitive data.

Scholarship Scams

In this type of phishing attack, attackers pose as scholarship organizations or institutions, offering scholarships to students who provide their personal information, such as social security numbers or banking details. Once the attackers have the information, they can use it for fraudulent activities.

Ransomware

Like any company, schools are also vulnerable to ransomware attacks, where malicious software encrypts school data and demands payment to restore access to the data. But that's always some other school district that doesn't have the security and process that your school is running, right? Here're some school districts, both large and small, that got hit with ransomware attacks in just the last 2 years. Think about how your district would be able to recover from this type of attack.

In May 2023, the FBI and CISA issued a joint advisory to warn that the Bl00dy Ransomware gang is now also actively exploiting a PaperCut remote-code execution vulnerability to gain initial access to education networks.

The U.S. Cybersecurity & Infrastructure Security Agency mentions that the threat actor has focused their attacks on the education sector, which has a significant public exposure of the flaw.

"In early May 2023, according to FBI information, the Bl00dy Ransomware Gang gained access to victim networks across the Education Facilities Subsector where PaperCut servers vulnerable to CVE-2023–27350 were exposed to the internet," reads the security advisory.

In May 2023, weeks after a cyberattack crippled the San Bernardino County Sheriff's Department computer systems, county officials confirmed that the hackers had been paid a $1.1-million ransom.

The ransomware attack, discovered in early April, forced the department to temporarily shut down some of its computer systems, including email, in-car computers and some law enforcement databases, including a system that deputies use for background checks.

After negotiating with the hackers, San Bernardino County paid slightly less than half the total —

$511,852—and its insurance carrier covered the rest, said county spokesman David Wert.

According to recent reports, the amount of ransomware payments made by schools and public sector organizations has been steadily increasing in recent years. In 2020, it was estimated that the total amount of ransomware payments made by schools and universities in the United States was more than $1.8 million.

Additionally, a number of school districts have reported that they have paid ransoms ranging from tens of thousands to hundreds of thousands of dollars to regain access to their systems and data.

It's important to note that paying a ransom only encourages and supports cybercriminals, and it is generally not recommended as a solution to ransomware attacks.

Don't let your digital transformation become a nightmare of ransomware and dollars paid.

Also, your IT department is aware that a robust Backup and Disaster Recovery plan should be able to mitigate vulnerability from ransomware. By archiving backups from different time-frames, defined by Recovery Point and Recovery Time Objectives (RPO & RTO), these archives could be the key to recovering from such a potential disaster.

Also be advised, if the ransomware or malware becomes embedded in your backups, your backups may include the virus. BEWARE!

Inadequate Security Measures

The author understands that it's not enough to say security measures are inadequate. In fact, you might say, ALL security measures are inadequate to stop ALL possible attacks, but it's only due diligence for each school district's IT department to license current software to address the relevant Cybersecurity threats.

By licensing it as a service, it will automatically be maintained and upgraded to the best ability of that service provider. This is one key example where paying for the monthly service includes SLAs and updates to address the latest and most dangerous viruses and malware in circulation.

Not only does your school's network require expensive network equipment and software, such as firewalls, antivirus software, and intrusion detection systems, they need to be managed, monitored and kept up-to-date. This means operational staff, dedicated to these roles.

Many of the school district IT departments known personally by the author are understaffed, and over tasked. Following are some of the most common types of inadequate cybersecurity measures affecting schools:

- Many schools do not regularly update their software, leaving vulnerabilities in their systems that hackers can exploit.
- Many schools do not use multi-factor authentication, which adds an extra layer of security by requiring users to provide additional information to access their accounts.

- Many schools do not provide sufficient cybersecurity training and awareness to their staff and students, leaving them vulnerable to phishing attacks and other cyber threats.
- Many schools have poor network segmentation, which allows hackers to move laterally across the network and gain access to sensitive data.
- Many schools do not have adequate data backup and disaster recovery plans in place, making it difficult to recover from a cyber attack.

Lack of Cybersecurity Training

School staff and students may not be aware of the latest cybersecurity threats and how to protect themselves from them. As part of your school's digital transformation efforts, be sure to identify and support the methods and processes adopted by your school's IT department, and reinforce them with all departments and users.

School districts should provide cybersecurity training to staff and students to help them understand the importance of cybersecurity and to develop good cybersecurity practices. As part of their agreement to access these services via the school's network and infrastructure, all users should be diligently informed through training via their AUP, email and websites.

The cybersecurity training and practices should be available on your district's IT website, part of an annual cybersecurity briefing and sent periodically to all users on a regular basis. You can't train your users too much.

Here are some of the key topics that should be covered in cybersecurity training for staff and students.

Strong Password Standards

Password standards are not requisite in all secure environments but good password maintenance and practice could be the key to securing your school's network. This should include training on how to create strong passwords, how to avoid using the same password for multiple accounts, and how to safely store and manage passwords.

Single Sign On

The need for multiple logins and passwords is a side-effect of digital transformation. Some school districts attempt to mitigate some of these side-effects with single sign-on services (SSO) but these systems can also be complicated to maintain and support.

Phishing Schemes

Understanding phishing schemes and the realization that most phishing schemes come via email, your district should include training on how to identify phishing emails, how to avoid clicking on suspicious links or downloading attachments from unknown sources, and how to report suspicious emails.

Some companies implement phishing awareness emails to test their users. In schools, IT departments should consider implementing similar testing for their administration and teaching staff.

Secure Browsing Habits

Users should be trained on secure internet browsing including how to avoid downloading malware, how to use a virtual private network (VPN) to protect internet traffic, and how to recognize and avoid malicious websites. A lot of this can be addressed proactively in the school environment using Internet filtering services. But even these are not foolproof and periodic training is still necessary.

Smart Device Security

Users should be trained on fundamentals of device security. This should include training on how to keep devices up-to-date with the latest software updates and security patches, how to secure mobile devices with strong passwords and encryption, and how to report lost or stolen devices.

Fortunately, this is an area that can be managed by the district's IT department through Mobile Device Management (MDM) and other software update and management platforms that should exist in the school's enterprise network. Whether the students are given iPads, Chromebooks, or Windows PCs, MDM should be implemented to secure all school-based computing devices.

BYOD Security

With your school's digital transformation, it is more important than ever for schools to implement BYOD security measures. With students bringing their own devices to school, it is essential that schools have a plan in place to protect student data and keep students safe online. These are implemented with your district's WIFI control and management systems.

There are a number of different BYOD security measures that schools can implement. Some common measures include:

Mobile Device Management (MDM) Systems

MDM systems allow schools to manage and secure mobile devices, such as smartphones and tablets. This is relevant for both district provided devices as well as BYOD devices. MDM systems can be used to enforce security policies, such as password requirements and app restrictions. For example, an MDM system can be used to require students to use strong passwords for their devices and to block them from installing certain apps.

Network Access Control (NAC) Systems

NAC systems allow schools to control who has access to the WIFI network. NAC systems can be used to block unauthorized devices from accessing the network. For example, a NAC system can be used to block devices that do not have the correct software installed or that are not registered with the school.

Web Filtering Systems

Web filtering systems allow schools to block access to certain websites and apps. This can help to protect students from harmful content, such as pornography or cyberbullying. For example, a web filtering system can be used to block access to websites that contain explicit content or that promote violence.

Data Encryption

Data encryption scrambles data so that it cannot be read by unauthorized users. This can help to protect student data from being stolen or hacked. For example, data encryption can be used to protect student grades and other sensitive information.

Data Breaches

Schools store sensitive information, including student and staff data, which can be targeted by hackers looking to steal personal information.

Clark County School District—In August 2020, the Clark County School District in Nevada reported a data breach that affected the personal information of approximately 370,000 students, staff, and alumni.

The group behind the Clark County School District's security breach claims to have uploaded all of the stolen data to its website—including information on current and former employees such as names and Social Security numbers. A Wall Street Journal report said the published data includes student names and grades and was published because the ransom demanded by the group had not been paid.

The San Diego Unified School District confirmed in October 2022, new details regarding the timeline of its "cybersecurity incident" in a report it filed with the state Attorney General's office.

The district "determined that the stolen data may include [a person's] name, Social Security number, health plan information, and/or direct deposit information." The district stated, it had been determined "that the data involved includes personal information of many current and former employees who have been employed with the district since 2020."

We can only guess how many identity thefts or other malicious attacks might have originated from these data breaches. These lists of people's names, addresses, and social security numbers are sold to malintents all over the world.

Distributed Denial of Service Attacks (DDOS)

Distributed Denial of Service (DDoS) attacks involve overwhelming a network or website with traffic to the point of rendering it inaccessible. K-12 schools are potential targets of DDoS attacks, which can disrupt online learning platforms, school websites, and other critical systems.

The New York Times reported on Monday, September of 2020, the first day of public school in Miami-Dade County, Florida, the fourth largest in the United States, students logged on to their virtual classrooms and immediately encountered slowness. Networks might typically have slowness or delays during the morning and afternoon class start times, but this was much more severe than normal.

The district's IT network seemed to be overwhelmed with traffic, students were getting error messages and other technical difficulties that lasted for days.

On Thursday, school administrators said that the problems had stemmed from cyberattacks—and that a 16-year-old student at South Miami Senior High School had been arrested.

"The student admitted to orchestrating eight Distributed Denial-of-Service cyberattacks, designed to overwhelm district networks," the district said in a statement. The student was charged as a juvenile offender with computer use in an attempt to defraud, a felony, and interference with an educational institution, a misdemeanor, the authorities said.

These types of attacks are where a large number of compromised devices, known as bots or zombies, flood a targeted system or network with traffic in order to overwhelm it and render it inaccessible. This is done by overwhelming the system's resources, such as its bandwidth, processing power, or memory, with a flood of requests or traffic, making it impossible for legitimate users to access the system.

DDoS attacks can be launched in various ways, but generally involves one or more attackers using a network of computers or other internet-connected devices that have been compromised through malware, phishing, or other methods. Schools present perfect circumstances for large numbers of non- or semi-secured internet-connected devices.

These compromised devices are then used to generate a massive amount of traffic that is directed towards the target system or network. The traffic generated by a DDoS attack can take many forms, such as null data packets, data requests, or false connection requests.

This flood of traffic can come from a variety of sources, including botnets, which are networks of infected computers that can be controlled remotely by an attacker, as well as spoofed IP addresses, which can make it difficult to trace the origin of the attack.

DDoS attacks can have a variety of motivations, including financial gain, political activism, revenge, or simply the desire to cause chaos or disruption. They can also be used as a diversionary tactic to distract security personnel while another attack is launched.

To defend against DDoS attacks, schools must implement a variety of techniques, including deploying dedicated hardware or software solutions, filtering traffic to block malicious requests, or contracting with cloud-based services that can absorb and mitigate the effects of a DDoS attack. The key to successful digital transformation is to have a comprehensive DDoS protection strategy in place that includes both proactive measures and reactive response plans as well as a comprehensive business continuity and disaster recovery plan. Just ask your IT director.

Internet of Things (IoT) Devices

Schools are also increasingly using IoT devices, such as smartboards, energy management systems, paging speakers, vape sensors, and IP-based security cameras, which may not be secure and can be easily hacked.

In 2019, a school district in New York was hit by a ransomware attack that encrypted the district's HVAC system, resulting in the district paying a ransom to regain control of the system.

In 2020, a school in Florida had its security camera system hacked by a cybercriminal who used the cameras to spy on classrooms and students. Security researchers found a vulnerability in a smart speaker used in classrooms that allowed them to remotely access the device and listen in on conversations.

In 2018, a school district in Indiana had its smart locks hacked, which allowed an intruder to gain access to the school.

These examples show how IoT devices, including HVAC systems, security cameras, smart speakers, and smart locks, can be vulnerable to cyberattacks in schools. It's important for schools to take proactive measures to secure their IoT devices, including implementing strong passwords, regularly updating software, and conducting security audits to identify and address vulnerabilities.

Once again, we're finding that just as much bad as good, can come from digital transformation. The key is to understand the current cybersecurity environment and your district's cybersecurity posture. Is your IT department being proactive as it works with your facilities and maintenance departments as they implement these systems?

Cyberbullying

Cyberbullying is a growing problem in schools, and is particularly focused on the students. With their constant use of social media and messaging apps, these platforms become the primary vehicle to socialize, collaborate, and spread news, but these interactions also sometimes turn to harassment and intimidation.

Not only has there been cyberbullying on general use apps such as Facebook and Instagram, but there've been many examples of cyberbullying on school district provided platforms such as Blackboard, Moodle and other LMSs.

Cyberbullying can have long-lasting and devastating effects on students' mental health, academic performance, and social well-being. Collaborative platforms provided by school districts should be used for positive communication and collaboration among students, teachers, and administrators, not for malicious or harmful behavior.

Oftentimes these interactions start off innocent and even helpful. But once students detect that no one is monitoring the platform, comments can become more personal and derogatory. If left without reporting or backlash, other students might join in the discussion, which in the end become cyberbullying.

These events can be devastating in high school as every grade counts towards the grade point average (GPA). If a cyberbullying incident affects the outcome of one grade, it could drop students from that target 5.0 (or 4.0) grade point average, which can ultimately impact a student's college eligibility—especially for top colleges and scholarship opportunities.

Here's some examples of different types of cyberbullying that may be happening in your school today:

Harassment

Sending mean or threatening messages, emails, or comments to the victim repeatedly. This can start out as constructive criticism, but left unreviewed, can easily escalate to harassment.

Teachers should monitor collaboration boards daily and discuss the particular symptoms that can lead to harassment openly with students. Teachers should also ask students to help call out questionable exchanges before it escalates to full blown harassment.

Keep in mind that almost any online interaction can escalate to harassment. Single comments which might seem innocent, can be harassment if the student on the receiving end feels ostracized, diminished or singled out.

Students are quick to develop code words, or seemingly innocent slang that is used to harass others in plain view of monitors and teachers. Students must be educated in what type of behavior can become harassment and help identify and report.

The school must implement anonymous reporting methods to help protect all involved. This might include students, parents and even others outside of the school. They may need to commit to some level of anonymity when reporting in order to foster trust and confidence in their student's own safety and security.

Impersonation

Impersonation is a very dangerous but common form of cyberbullying. Creating fake social media profiles or using someone else's identity to humiliate or harm the victim. This has not only been identified between students within classrooms, but even with students outside the classroom or school, and even with parents impersonating their own children, in their defense—or attacking other students as revenge.

This type of cyberbullying could be very difficult to identify and zero-in on the culprit. Students might use any type of method to steal another student's credentials and then begin sabotaging their work. Again, one incident can permanently injure or completely destroy another student's academic career and even personal life.

Parental tendencies to help and protect their children become the impetus to act on their behalf. In fact, there have been many Lifetime movies based on true stories detailing how parents have taken over and impersonated their own students. Some of these stories have had the worst-case outcomes.

Parents often gain their student's online credentials for many reasons, sometimes to help with college applications and other social or academic activities. But once in their accounts, they become privy to their student's private conversations and academic history. Most full-featured LMS systems include alternate credentials for parents. That way the parents can access their student's accounts, but cannot act on their behalf.

Exclusion

A more passive form of cyberbullying is exclusion, intentionally leaving someone out of group chats, collaboration activities or social events online. This can manifest as bullying or sabotage. In one example, a team project is a collaboration, but by omitting one of the team members in communications, their participation is hindered or excluded, resulting in poor results for the individual.

Rumors

One of the most common forms of cyberbullying is the spreading of false or damaging rumors about someone through social media or messaging apps. This is obvious, but also enabled through both common apps as well as education focused platforms. In some cases, the platform can become the proof of cyberbullying, thus the teachers and providers of these platforms must accept the responsibility of policing these platforms.

Once again, these interactions may begin with helpful critique or collaboration but then turn into cyberbullying just by participating and / or proliferating untruths.

Public shaming

Shaming is the cyber version of the stocks. Posting embarrassing pictures or videos of someone without their consent. Within the school, there's ample opportunity to capture pictures or videos of others since every single tablet, laptop, smartphone has a camera. Posting pictures of others without their consent should be specifically banned in schools' acceptable use policies (AUP) and students are well advised to understand the implications and impacts.

Comments, screenshots of incorrect answers, and compromising pictures can all be artifacts of public shaming. Students may think that sharing an embarrassing snapshot is innocent enough but could be the final straw for a student suffering from social or psychological issues.

Doxing

Doxing has been widely reported in the general public as it has proven dangerous and even deadly when someone's confidential address is revealed to the public. When protestors and activists show up to protest in front of a judge or congressperson's home.

Also, the act of SWATing (calling the police and reporting armed invaders to cause the SWAT team to show up at an innocent person's home) can have terrible outcomes. Revealing someone's personal information online without their permission is always wrong and one of the most destructive forms of cyberbullying.

In light of all these examples, school districts should proactively implement robust policies and procedures to prevent cyberbullying, and ensure that students, teachers, and parents are educated about the risks and consequences of such behavior. In case of any incidents, proper channels of reporting and investigation should be in place to ensure that the situation is dealt with promptly and effectively.

As a district, it is now requisite that a consolidated front be presented to address any and all incidents of cyberbullying. School districts should create clear policies regarding cyberbullying and educate students, parents, and staff about the rules and consequences of such behavior. It is important to enforce these policies consistently to prevent further instances of cyberbullying.

The first incidence of cyberbullying is every school's opportunity to address this immediately and publicly. Ask yourself, when has (or has) leadership addressed the district's policy response to incidents of cyberbullying? How was it received? Was it successful? How was this opportunity leveraged?

School districts should establish a safe and anonymous reporting mechanism that allows students and staff to report incidents of cyberbullying. It is important that these reports are taken seriously, investigated promptly, and that the victim's privacy is protected throughout the process.

School districts should partner with community organizations, such as local law enforcement and mental health providers, to address cyberbullying beyond its own walls. These partnerships can provide additional resources and expertise to address the issue.

These subjects should be discussed first in leadership and cabinet meetings to initially raise awareness and priority by district leadership. Only by addressing this directly, from the mouth of the superintendent, will administration and teaching staff understand the importance of developing and enforcing anti-cyberbullying policies.

As part of any digital transformation initiative, school districts should prioritize a positive school culture that values respect, empathy, and inclusivity. Creating a positive environment can help prevent cyberbullying and encourage students to speak up when they see it happening.

Enforcement

Whenever we discuss acceptable use policies and cyberbullying, the next obvious questions pertain to enforcement and penalties. What can be done when students ignore and disobey these policies. What types of enforcement are applicable? What type of punishment or accountability will be acceptable?

First start with educating students about the various forms of cyberbullying and their potential negative effects on individuals and the school. We've already discussed how schools should implement educational programs to teach students about the negative effects of cyberbullying and how to prevent it.

Policies and procedures should be documented and published for administration and staff. Schools must have policies that prohibit cyberbullying and establish consequences for students who engage in such behavior. These policies can include disciplinary action, such as detention, suspension, or expulsion, depending on the severity of the incident.

Staff should receive training specific to how to identify and respond to cyberbullying incidents. This can include how to report incidents to appropriate authorities, how to support victims, and how to address cyberbullying in the classroom.

Schools must provide resources for students who are victims of cyberbullying, such as counseling services, support groups, or access to mental health professionals.

And of course, the holistic approach must include the family at home. Schools' efforts to combat cyberbullying should involve parents by providing periodic communications and resources for how to identify and prevent cyberbullying, reporting procedures, and by notifying parents if their child is involved in a cyberbullying incident.

Remote Learning Security

COVID-19 turned the world, including the world of K-12 Education, upside-down. Only now are our heads finally starting to settle from the dead zone that was 2020 and 2021. Schools were thrust head-first into the chaos of online learning—without proper preparation.

Yes, some schools and individuals that were focused on moving toward online learning already had a head start. But for the most part, the front line soldiers (the teachers) were burdened with the major forklifting of their curriculum into the ether. Most without the thought of online pedagogy and online curriculum.

Online pedagogy involves the use of digital technologies to deliver educational content and facilitate learning. It includes various teaching strategies such as online lectures, discussion forums, virtual simulations, and multimedia resources that are accessible from anywhere and at any time. Online pedagogy can be used to supplement or replace traditional classroom instruction, offering greater flexibility and accessibility for learners. As always, online pedagogy is teacher-centric. AI will never take their place.

Major Cybersecurity Trends in Education

As schools increasingly move to cloud-based solutions for storage and collaboration, securing internal network and cloud services has become a major focus for cybersecurity in education. Here are a few of the industry trends and best practices your school district should have or be implementing.

Multi-Factor Authentication

Multi-factor authentication (MFA) is becoming more common in schools, requiring users to provide multiple forms of identification before accessing sensitive data. This may entail loading special apps on smartphones, email verification, having a security key device, and even having to receive phone calls, in order to provide additional verification. With these additional steps, Single Sign-On (SSO) becomes an important service that should be implemented district-wide to help simplify passwords.

IoT Security

Internet of Things (IoT) devices are becoming more prevalent in schools, and securing these devices has become a major challenge. Schools need to ensure that IoT devices are properly configured, updated, and secured to prevent unauthorized access.

Most of these devices have been installed by school district facilities management departments as Point of Sale (POS), Energy Management, Access Control and Facilities management systems. But some IoT devices like refrigerators and microwaves might be getting installed in your school network as well.

These systems are arguably just as important as student information and payroll, yet they've come onto the network without a lot of the security features necessary in today's chaotic network.

Once Again, TRAINING

As the human element remains a weak point in cybersecurity, security awareness training is becoming more important in education. Schools are increasingly providing cybersecurity education and training to staff and students to help them identify and prevent cyber threats. Obviously, staff, who have access to confidential servers and data should receive specific training to address not only what can be at risk, but the many ways their own awareness and activities can impact cyber threats.

As schools recognize, acknowledge, and become more aware of the risks posed by cyber threats, IT departments must develop an incident response plan to minimize opportunities and mitigate the impact of cyber incidents. These plans outline procedures for responding to cyber incidents and mitigating their effects.

Cybersecurity in Schools and Zero Trust

Zero trust is a security model that assumes all users and devices, whether inside or outside the network, are potential threats and should not be trusted by default. Instead, access to resources is granted on a need-to-know basis, and authentication and authorization are continuously verified. Implementing zero trust can help to protect against cyber attacks and data breaches.

Zero trust can be implemented in K-12 data centers as well as district-wide to enhance security and protect against cyber threats. Implementing zero trust can improve support for digital transformation in K-12 schools in several ways. It can help to secure one of the most obvious vulnerabilities that most schools suffer from, secure remote access.

With the rise of remote learning and hybrid learning models, many K-12 schools have adopted remote access solutions to enable students and staff to access district resources from anywhere. Zero trust can help to secure remote access by verifying user and device identity and ensuring that only authorized users and devices are granted access to resources. This can help to protect against unauthorized access and reduce the risk of data breaches. But be ready to purchase and install some new hardware and software licenses to support this. It's not cheap, and it doesn't run by itself. By now, your district should have a designated cybersecurity resource, this will be part of their job.

Zero trust can help to reduce the complexity of network management by eliminating the need for complex network segmentation and access control policies.

By simplifying network management, K-12 schools can improve network performance and reduce the risk of human error. So, zero trust not only provides the highest level of network security, but also provides tools to better monitor and manage networks systems and services.

By implementing strict access controls and continuously verifying user and device identity, zero trust implementation reduces the risk of unauthorized access and minimizes the impact of security incidents. This can help to protect against cyber attacks and data breaches, which can be costly and damaging to the reputation of the school.

There are several technologies that can be used to implement zero trust in K-12 data centers and district-wide, including identity and access management (IAM) solutions, multi-factor authentication (MFA), network segmentation, Data loss prevention (DLP) systems monitor data flows and prevent sensitive data from being exfiltrated from the network.

Security information and event management (SIEM) systems collect and analyze security logs from across the network to identify potential threats.

Threat intelligence provides organizations with information about known threats, such as malicious IP addresses and domains. Vulnerability management tools scan systems for known vulnerabilities and help organizations to prioritize and remediate those vulnerabilities.

By implementing these technologies, schools can create a more secure and resilient network infrastructure that can support their digital transformation initiatives.

Cybersecurity Incident Response

Cybersecurity incidents can be disruptive, costly, and potentially damaging to the reputation of the school district. An incident response plan provides a structured approach to managing and mitigating the impact of cybersecurity incidents, and can help to minimize the risks and costs associated with such incidents.

An effective incident response plan should include procedures for detecting and reporting cybersecurity incidents, as well as guidelines for containing, analyzing, and remedying the incident. The plan should also include steps for communicating with stakeholders such as students, staff, and parents, and for notifying law enforcement and other relevant authorities as necessary.

Given the sensitive nature of student and staff data held by school districts, it is particularly important for school districts to have an incident response plan in place. The plan should include procedures for protecting data in the event of a breach, as well as guidelines for restoring services and systems in the aftermath of an incident.

Here are some common steps that lay out the development of a K-12 school-specific incident response plan:

Establish a Response Team

Identify the key personnel who will be involved in responding to a cybersecurity incident, such as the IT director, key engineers, impacted school administrators, and district legal counsel.

Selecting the right individuals for a cybersecurity response team in a typical school district is crucial to ensure effective incident response. The process typically involves identifying the necessary cybersecurity skills based on the type of security incident, and assessing the availability of staff members who can commit to the role while maintaining their regular job responsibilities.

Interested staff members who meet the necessary skills and availability requirements are invited to submit applications and resumes, and selected applicants are interviewed to assess their experience, skills, and enthusiasm for the role.

Technical skills required for a cybersecurity response team member include knowledge of operating systems, programming languages, security tools, and other technical concepts related to cybersecurity. An in-depth understanding of network protocols, infrastructure, and data analysis tools is also essential to detect and respond to cybersecurity incidents.

Familiarity with intrusion detection and prevention systems, firewalls, antivirus software, and other security tools is also critical to effectively respond to incidents. In addition, members of a cybersecurity response team should have an understanding of cybersecurity frameworks and regulations, such as the NIST Cybersecurity Framework, HIPAA, and FERPA, that are applicable to their organization.

Create an Incident Response Plan

Develop a plan that outlines the steps that will be taken in the event of a cybersecurity incident, including communication channels, roles and responsibilities, and escalation procedures. Following is a simple example of a Cybersecurity Incident Response Plan.

Identification

In case of a cybersecurity incident, the first step is to identify the incident and its scope. This can be done through the use of security tools, network monitoring, or reports from employees or other sources.

Based on the type of incident, the response team must identify the engineer most qualified to lead the forensic assessment and help identify the source and / or cause of the incident, the virus or malware involved, and necessary tools and services to aid in problem resolution.

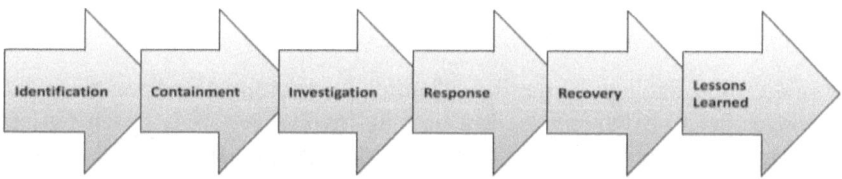

Figure 4.1 Cybersecurity Incident Response Plan

Containment

Once the incident has been identified, the next step is to contain it to prevent further damage or spread of the attack. This may involve disconnecting affected systems from the network or shutting down compromised servers. It may also require deployment of special anti-virus software and / or services.

Containment measures are an essential part of any incident response plan. These measures are designed to limit the impact of a cybersecurity incident and prevent it from spreading to other systems or data.

Isolating affected systems is one of the most effective ways to contain an incident, as it prevents the attacker from accessing other systems or data. Blocking malicious traffic and disabling compromised user accounts are also important measures to limit the attacker's ability to spread the incident.

In addition to these measures, implementing network segmentation can help isolate critical systems and data from the rest of the network. This can be especially useful in preventing the spread of incidents involving malware or other types of attacks. Containing malware is another important aspect of incident response, as it can help prevent the attacker from controlling affected systems or stealing sensitive data.

It's important to note that effective containment measures require a thorough understanding of the incident and the organization's security posture. This includes identifying the scope and severity of the incident, as well as understanding the organization's network topology and the location of critical systems and data. In some cases, it may be necessary to involve external experts such as cybersecurity consultants or law enforcement agencies to help contain the incident.

Investigation

After the incident has been contained, a forensic assessment investigation should be conducted to determine the root cause of the incident and assess the extent of the damage. This may involve analyzing logs, reviewing network traffic, interviewing affected personnel, and gathering all the data from the investigation for the incident report. Even the symptoms and troubleshooting methodology will be important later on. The investigative sequence of events may inform future incidents.

Response

Based on the findings of the investigation, an appropriate response should be developed and implemented. This may involve restoring systems from backups, applying security patches or updates, or implementing new security measures.

Any time your IT department calls in an incident or trouble call, the analyst will ask if all the patches and operating systems are up to date. That means that the primary mitigation factor might simply be to keep software up to date and security patches installed as prescribed by the manufacturer.

Recovery

Once the incident has been resolved, efforts should be made to restore normal business operations as quickly as possible. This may involve conducting additional testing, providing training to employees, or implementing additional security measures to prevent future incidents.

One of the most important recovery measures is restoring data from backups. This can help ensure that critical data is not lost due to the incident. However, it's important to ensure that the backup data is not also compromised before restoring it. Applying security patches and updates to affected systems is another important mitigation measure, as it can help prevent the attacker from exploiting known vulnerabilities in the future.

Mitigation

Once the recovery is complete, additional plans should be made to implement changes and deploy tools to prevent further similar incidents or attacks.

Mitigation measures are another important aspect of incident response that aim to reduce the lasting impact of a cybersecurity incident. These measures are focused on restoring affected systems and data, as well as implementing additional security controls to prevent similar incidents from occurring in the future. Once again, mitigation might be more training.

Implementing additional security controls, such as intrusion detection and prevention systems, firewalls, and endpoint security solutions, can also help prevent future incidents. Conducting a thorough post-incident analysis is an important step in mitigation, as it helps identify the root cause of the incident and provide information on how to improve the organization's security posture.

Communicate with Stakeholders

Communicate with key stakeholders, such as parents, staff, and law enforcement, about the incident, its impact, and the steps being taken to mitigate it.

As always, communication is the key. Communication to all stakeholders must be immediate and complete. It must provide a detailed description of what happened, the criticality of the event (number of users impacted), the root cause analysis, what was done to resolve the issue and what was done to prevent a recurrence of the attack.

It should also state who was responsible (if known), and what enforcement policies were implemented. Here's a sample communications your Cybersecurity Incident Response team can use as a template.

Dear Stakeholders,

We would like to inform you about a cybersecurity incident that occurred on our network. On [date/time], we discovered an unauthorized access attempt to our system. As a precautionary measure, we immediately activated our cybersecurity incident response plan to identify and contain the incident.

Our cybersecurity team worked diligently to investigate and contain the incident. After conducting a thorough investigation, we can confirm that no data was stolen or compromised. However, there may have been a brief period where access to certain systems or services was interrupted as we worked to contain the incident.

We take cybersecurity very seriously and have implemented measures to mitigate the risks of future incidents. We are also conducting a review of our existing cybersecurity policies and procedures to identify areas for improvement.

We would like to assure you that we have taken steps to prevent a similar incident from happening in the future. We value your trust and remain committed to ensuring the security and privacy of your data.

If you have any concerns or questions, please do not hesitate to contact us at [contact information]. We appreciate your understanding and support during this incident.

Sincerely,

XYZ School District Cybersecurity Response Team

Lessons Learned

Finally, it is important to document the incident response process, including any lessons learned, and to incorporate these into future incident response plans. This will help to improve the effectiveness of the organization's cybersecurity incident response capabilities over time.

Just as a problem management database expands with each problem resolved, the same is true for cybersecurity incident and event management (SIEM) database.

Educate Staff and Students

Cybersecurity in schools is becoming increasingly important as more and more school systems move towards digital education. Staff and students need to be aware of the fundamental aspects of cybersecurity to ensure that their school's networks and data are secure. Most of the cybersecurity threats relevant to schools have already been discussed. For this part of your school's incident response plan, be sure to train teachers and students on the fundamentals.

The following are some key concepts that staff and students should be made aware of:
- Use of Strong Passwords
- Identifying Phishing email scams
- Protecting personally identifiable information (PII)
- K-12 education targeted threats: credit card, scholarship, and financial aid scams
- Staff and students should be made aware of the risks associated with social media.

Monitor Systems & Managed Services

The district IT department should have a suite of cybersecurity monitoring tools. Either by implementing them on premise, or leveraging services offered by Managed Service Providers (MSPs). Also, Security Information and Event Management (SIEM), and Business Continuity and Disaster Recovery (BCDR) services are all applicable to schools and can play a significant role in improving their cybersecurity posture.

Since most school districts don't have the FTE count for 2–3 more cybersecurity analysts MSPs become the only logical solution. Here's how each of these services can be beneficial for schools:

Managed Service Providers are third-party companies that provide a range of IT services, such as network management, software updates, and cybersecurity. MSPs offer service plans that help schools manage their IT infrastructure, implement security controls, and monitor for cybersecurity threats. This can be especially helpful for schools that may not have the resources or expertise to manage their own cybersecurity.

Security Information and Event Management (SIEM) is a technology that helps organizations monitor their network for security incidents and respond to them in real-time. SIEM can be especially helpful for schools that have a large number of users and devices on their network, as it can help identify potential security incidents before they become major problems.

Business Continuity and Disaster Recovery (BCDR) services help organizations prepare for and recover from unexpected events, such as natural disasters or cyber-attacks. BCDR can be especially helpful for schools as it can help them recover critical systems and data in the event of an outage or attack.

BCDR is also one the often neglected services of most IT departments. Yes, they may be running their backups, but when was the last time they tested a recovery? Can they do partial recoveries? What is the frequency of your district's disaster recovery testing?

These are all questions that may point your district towards engaging with an MSP for these critical services. And when your IT director comes to you with this alphabet soup, MSP, SIEM, BCDR, remember, it is well worth the cost.

Privacy and Compliance

Schools are subject to a range of privacy and compliance regulations, including FERPA and GDPR (EU). Ensuring compliance with these regulations has become a top priority in cybersecurity in education.

Yes, many of these cybersecurity platforms and standards are applicable to schools, as schools also handle sensitive data, such as student and employee information. Here are some examples:

NIST Cybersecurity Framework

The NIST Cybersecurity Framework is applicable to schools as it provides a framework for managing and reducing cybersecurity risk, which is essential for protecting sensitive information.

CIS Controls

The CIS Controls are also applicable to schools, as they provide a set of best practices for information security. By implementing these controls, schools can improve their cybersecurity posture and protect their sensitive data.

HIPAA

Although HIPAA is typically associated with healthcare organizations, it can also be applicable to schools that handle student health information, such as medical records.

FERPA

The Family Educational Rights and Privacy Act (FERPA) is a U.S. federal law that protects the privacy of student education records. Schools that receive federal funding are required to comply with FERPA.

COPPA

The Children's Online Privacy Protection Act (COPPA) is a U.S. federal law that regulates the collection and use of personal information from children under the age of 13. Schools that collect personal information from children under the age of 13 must comply with COPPA.

Cybersecurity Services

There are many other cybersecurity services and solutions that can be beneficial for schools. Here are a few examples:

Endpoint Security

Endpoint security solutions help protect individual devices, such as laptops, desktops, and mobile devices, from cyber threats. This is especially important for schools that have a large number of devices on their network. Endpoint security solutions can help detect and prevent malware infections, unauthorized access, and other security threats.

Cloud Security

Many schools are moving their data and applications to the cloud, which can provide cost savings and improved accessibility. However, cloud environments also introduce new security challenges. Cloud security solutions help organizations secure their data and applications in the cloud, including protecting against unauthorized access, data breaches, and other security threats.

Firewall and Intrusion Detection/Prevention Systems (IDS/IPS)

Firewalls and IDS/IPS solutions help organizations protect their network from unauthorized access and cyber-attacks. These solutions can help detect and prevent malicious traffic from entering the network, and can also help identify potential security incidents in real-time.

CYBERSECURITY INCIDENT REPORTING

What is a cybersecurity incident? In the IT world, an incident is anything that slows down or interrupts operations and production. With the word cybersecurity preceding, the incident is now related to technology systems in the organization. Which is the lifeblood of the organization. So . . .

K-12 Schools should implement cybersecurity incident reporting for several reasons.

Incident reporting helps prepare schools to respond to future cybersecurity incidents in a timely and efficient manner. Early detection and reporting of incidents can help minimize the damage caused and prevent further spread of the incident. Other schools may benefit from your team's reporting and response.

Incident reporting provides valuable data for conducting a root cause analysis of the incident. This analysis can help schools identify the underlying cause of the incident and take appropriate measures to prevent similar incidents in the future.

Many industries and organizations are required by law or regulation to report cybersecurity incidents. Failure to report incidents can result in legal or financial penalties, as well as damage to the district's reputation.

Incident reporting provides organizations with a feedback mechanism for improving their cybersecurity defenses. By analyzing incident reports, organizations can identify weaknesses in their security posture and take corrective action.

Incident reporting can facilitate information sharing among districts, enabling them to learn from each other's experiences and better defend against education focused cybersecurity threats.

Implementing a cybersecurity incident reporting system is crucial for schools to effectively manage and respond to cybersecurity incidents, mitigate the impact of incidents, and continuously improve their security posture.

The Cybersecurity Incident Report

Reporting cybersecurity incidents is essential for protecting schools from potential cyber threats. By reporting incidents, schools can identify the nature and scope of the attack and take immediate action to contain and mitigate its impact.

Reporting incidents also helps to create a culture of awareness and preparedness among staff and students. When incidents are reported, it provides an opportunity to educate and train employees on the importance of cybersecurity best practices.

Another important reason to report incidents is to comply with legal and regulatory requirements. Many industries, Healthcare, Finance and K-12 and Higher Education, are subject to strict data privacy and security regulations. Failing to report incidents can result in significant fines and reputational damage.

Lastly, reporting incidents can help schools to identify and address vulnerabilities in their security systems. By analyzing the causes of the incident and implementing changes to prevent similar attacks in the future, schools can strengthen their security posture and reduce the risk of future incidents.

THE KEY COMPONENTS OF A CYBERSECURITY INCIDENT REPORT INCLUDE:

Incident Summary

A brief description of the incident, including the date and time it occurred, the type of incident, and the impact on the organization. It should outline the response taken by the cybersecurity team, including any steps taken to contain and mitigate the impact of the incident. Additionally, the summary should include a review of the incident to identify any vulnerabilities in the organization's security systems.

Details of the Incident

A detailed description of the incident, including how it was detected, the systems or applications affected, the duration of the incident, and any sensitive data that was compromised. The details should include a chronology of events, including, the criticality of the incident (number of users impacted) and other time critical factors, such as escalation to third parties and other service providers.

This section should include technical details, such as the type of attack, the affected systems, and any indicators of compromise (IOCs) found during the investigation, the extent of the damage caused by the incident, including any data loss or theft, and the potential impact of the incident on the organization's operations, finances, and reputation.

Response to the Incident

A description of the steps taken to contain and remediate the incident, including the individuals or teams involved and any external assistance requested. What was the IT department's first knowledge of the incident? Through proactive monitoring and status reporting? Through alert status on performance monitoring? Through user trouble-call via the help desk?

How was the incident assigned to an IT resource? What were the first courses of action prescribed and taken? The more data available about how an incident was detected, reported, assigned and escalated will inform an assessment of the efficiency of incident detection and response. Which will become a metric for improvement in the future.

Resolution

A detailed explanation of the tasks performed to resolve the incident, such as patching software or hardware, identifying and remediating vulnerabilities, and implementing additional security measures.

How was the incident resolved?

In the case of a malware or ransomware attack, it may take days to identify and isolate the affected systems. Then recovery might require restoring from a backup or even paying a ransom. All the details of the activity and actions are important for reporting and forensic analysis.

You can see from this example that the recovery task was a restore from backups. Which begs the question, how much data was lost from the backup recovery point? And how do we know that the recovery point preceded the infection?

Root Cause Analysis

An explanation of the root cause of the incident, including any vulnerabilities or weaknesses that were exploited, and whether the incident could have been prevented.

This is the hindsight is 20/20 analysis. Once the incident has been resolved, and operations are restored, the RCA should provide all the remaining details of the source of the attack, the vulnerability exploited, and any human error or intervention that might have prevented the incident.

Mitigation

A detailed plan to prevent recurrence of the incident. What was the vulnerability? Was it addressed? What was the source? Has it been cleansed? How will we know if it has been mitigated?

These and other questions about proactive efforts by the IT department to 1) implement the recommended prevention and 2) identify other related vulnerabilities.

Lessons Learned

A description of the lessons learned from the incident, including any changes to policies or procedures that need to be made, and any improvements that can be made to incident response in the future.

CHAPTER FIVE

The Technical Side of Digital Transformation

DIGITAL TRANSFORMATION AND THE DISTRICT DATA CENTER

Digital transformation in K–12 education isn't limited to classrooms. In fact, depending on the computing architectures and infrastructure at your district, there could be a larger potential impact in your district's back-end computing systems and services. By making traditional computing environments and services obsolete, there's no telling how much time and resources might be wasted until an assessment is made.

Or more likely, an incidental digital transformation occurs that makes the improvement glaring. Like when your district went from whatever your old payroll systems to the current one. The author can assume that your district is on some web-based or hosted payroll and HR system that is cloud-based. Any school district that is still in the business of printing checks is in the dark ages—literally. Although some exceptions do exist.

One of the greatest recent technological leaps is called hyper-convergence.

HyperConverged Infrastructure and Data Center Digital Transformation

Hyperconvergence is an IT hardware architecture that combines compute, storage, and networking into a single, software-defined solution. Hyperconverged Infrastructure (HCI) is designed to simplify data center management by consolidating all the components of a traditional data center into a single, easy-to-manage system. In an HCI system, storage is delivered through a distributed file system, eliminating the need for a separate storage area network (SAN) or network-attached storage (NAS) device.

Think of the traditional computer architecture starting from the 1960s. First there was the mainframe computer that had a central processing unit, which might have been as big as a refrigerator. Users communicating to the CPU used terminals that connected to the CPU via simple wired connections.

The data was stored on large banks that were also the size of refrigerators and held layers of silicon-layered over non-conductive substrate disks. Data centers the size of football fields were needed to house hundreds and thousands of these refrigerator-sized cabinets to support the computing requirements of large companies and government agencies. They would be the only organizations that could afford such computing power. Only the largest school districts could afford these types of investments.

In the 1980s to 1990s we saw the personal computer become a client to the enterprise server and the network became an entity of its own using a technology called ethernet. Even the medium-sized school districts started building their own data centers and investing in data center server computers, if they could justify the need.

Through the early 2000s we saw large multi-processor servers accessing large storage-area networks (SANs) via local-area networks (LANs)—this was the era known as "Client-Server Architecture," and it sucked the financial investments of school districts from small to large. Along with the expansion of Wide-Area Networking (WANs) and of course, the development and explosion of the Internet and the concept of IoT.

Now take that enterprise computing architecture (Servers, LANs and SANs) and collapse them on one microprocessor. One multilayered fiberglass non-conductive substrate material printed with copper molecules layered to create a multi-processor that might have as many as 128 pentium processors and 100 terabytes of data storage on a single motherboard. This is hyperconvergence and if you replace all your current computing resources with this architecture, this is known as HyperConverged Infrastructure (HCI).

This approach simplifies data storage and management and reduces the amount of hardware needed to support the infrastructure. HCI is so dense, a computing architecture that might have taken multiple cabinets (those refrigerator-sized cabinets) to support, may now take one or two rack units (RUs) in a single computing cabinet. That single cabinet, however, will require expanded power and cooling within the data center.

Hyperconvergence also typically includes virtualization technology, allowing multiple virtual machines (VMs) to run on a single physical host. By combining compute, storage, and networking into a single system, HCI offers a more efficient and scalable way to manage IT resources.

Data center virtualization leveraging hyperconverged infrastructure (HCI) can play a crucial role in supporting digital transformation in K–12 schools. By simplifying the deployment and management of virtual machines and storage resources, HCI can improve efficiency and scalability in IT infrastructure. This can help K–12 schools easily adapt to the changing demands of digital learning without needing extensive IT resources.

Imagine the old computer-lab in each school with anywhere from 15 to 150 personal computers each with its own internal CPU, disk drive and network card. Now collapse all that computing power into one chip on one board on one rack unit (known as a RU). You could power enough student devices for a large school district in a box the size of a small college dorm refrigerator (to complete the refrigerator references).

Additionally, HCI can reduce costs associated with maintaining traditional data center infrastructure. With HCI, schools can avoid purchasing separate hardware for storage and networking, which can be expensive and time-consuming to manage. Instead, all resources are managed through a single console, reducing the need for specialized IT staff and simplifying infrastructure management.

HCI can also improve data security in K–12 schools. With HCI, sensitive data is stored in a centralized location and protected by advanced security measures. This can help protect student and staff information from cyber threats and unauthorized access.

While data center virtualization leveraging hyperconverged infrastructure (HCI) can support digital transformation in K–12 schools, its applicability may vary based on the size of the school district.

Large school districts often have complex IT infrastructures, with multiple schools and thousands of students and staff. In such cases, HCI can provide significant benefits by simplifying infrastructure management, improving scalability, and reducing costs. With HCI, large districts can centralize IT resources and provide a consistent learning experience to students across multiple schools.

On the other hand, smaller school districts may not have the same level of complexity in their IT infrastructure. They may have fewer schools and a smaller student population, making it easier to manage IT resources manually. In such cases, the benefits of HCI may not outweigh the costs of adoption.

Smaller school districts may also face budget constraints, which can make it difficult to invest in expensive IT infrastructure. They may prefer to invest in other areas, such as teacher training, curriculum development, or student resources.

Enterprise computing architectures using HCI can support digital transformation in schools by providing a flexible, scalable, and cost-effective IT infrastructure. One of the main benefits of HCI is simplified infrastructure management. By consolidating all necessary hardware and software resources into a single system, school IT staff can easily manage, update, and maintain the system. This simplifies the process of deploying and managing virtual machines and storage resources.

Another advantage of HCI is scalability. As schools grow and need to add more IT resources, HCI can easily accommodate those changes by adding more nodes to the system. This can help schools keep up with the increasing demand for digital learning tools and resources without needing to invest in separate hardware for storage and networking.

HCI can also help reduce costs associated with maintaining traditional data center infrastructure. By using a single system to manage all IT resources, schools can avoid purchasing separate hardware for storage and networking. This can be expensive and time-consuming to manage. Instead, all resources are managed through a single console, reducing the need for specialized IT staff and simplifying infrastructure management.

In addition, HCI can improve data security in schools. With HCI, sensitive data is stored in a centralized location and protected by advanced security measures. This can help protect student and staff information from cyber threats and unauthorized access.

Data Center Digital Transformation and the Cloud

Cloud computing can be a more cost-effective option for smaller school districts in digital transformation for several reasons. Firstly, it can reduce infrastructure costs. Smaller school districts with limited IT resources may not have the budget to purchase and maintain their own servers, storage, and networking equipment. With cloud computing, schools can access these resources through a cloud provider, which can significantly reduce hardware and maintenance costs. This can help smaller districts focus their resources on other areas, such as teacher training, curriculum development, or student resources.

Secondly, cloud computing can provide greater flexibility and scalability. As schools grow and need to add more resources, they can easily scale up their cloud resources to meet the increased demand. This allows smaller districts to adapt to changing needs and budgets without having to invest in expensive hardware upgrades or replacements.

Thirdly, cloud computing can offer access to a wider range of digital learning tools and resources. By leveraging cloud services, schools can access a variety of applications, software, and digital content, regardless of their location or IT infrastructure. This can help smaller districts provide their students with the same high-quality education and resources as larger districts, without needing to invest in expensive hardware or software licenses.

Finally, cloud computing can offer improved data security. Cloud providers typically have advanced security measures in place to protect against cyber threats and data breaches. This can help ensure that student and staff data is kept safe and secure, without requiring schools to invest in expensive security measures themselves.

Digital Transformation and the Software Defined Networking

Software-defined networking (SDN) is a technology that abstracts the control and management of the network from the underlying hardware, making it easier to manage and automate network resources. In the context of K–12 data centers, SDN can have a significant impact on digital transformation initiatives.

By separating the network from the underlying hardware, SDN enables administrators to manage and configure the network more efficiently, by reducing the time and resources required to identify issues, plan and implement changes.

SDN provides greater visibility into network performance and security, allowing administrators to identify and address issues more quickly.

SDN can support other digital transformation initiatives, such as cloud computing and virtualization. By providing a more agile and flexible network infrastructure, SDN can help schools to adopt new technologies and services more quickly and easily. For example, SDN can enable the automated deployment of virtual machines (VMs) and the dynamic allocation of network resources, making it easier to scale up or down as needed. This can be particularly beneficial in the context of virtual desktop infrastructure (VDI), where the network is critical to delivering a high-quality user experience.

There are several K–12 school districts that have implemented SDN to support their digital transformation initiatives. One example is the Beaverton School District in Oregon, which implemented SDN to improve network performance and security for its 40,000 students and 5,000 staff members. The district deployed an SDN solution, which provided centralized management and automation of network resources. The SDN solution allowed the district to improve network performance by dynamically allocating bandwidth to critical applications, such as video conferencing and online testing. In addition, the solution provided enhanced security features, such as network segmentation and threat detection, to protect against cyber threats.

Another example is the Hilliard City Schools district in Ohio, which implemented SDN to support its 16,000 students and 2,000 staff members. The district deployed an SDN solution, which provided a unified network architecture and simplified network management. The SDN solution enabled the

Digital Transformation and the Realm of Data Backup and Disaster Recovery

These issues are more relevant today than ever but unless you are the CTO of your district, this may never come up.

The era of digital transformation in K–12 schools has brought about significant changes in data backup and disaster recovery strategies. One of the most notable changes is the sheer amount of data that needs to be backed up. With the increasing use of digital resources in K–12 schools, the amount of data that needs to be protected has grown significantly. This includes student records, learning materials, and administrative data, all of which need to be backed up regularly to ensure they can be recovered in the event of a disaster.

Another change is the frequency of data backups. In the past, many schools may have only backed up their data once a week or even less frequently. However, with the increased reliance on digital resources, schools are now backing up their data more frequently, sometimes as often as every few hours. This ensures that the most up-to-date data is always available in the event of a disaster.

Additionally, schools are increasingly turning to cloud-based backup solutions. Cloud backup offers several benefits, including lower costs, greater scalability, and increased reliability. Cloud backup solutions also typically offer faster recovery times, which is critical in the event of a disaster. Schools can also benefit from the ability to access their backups from anywhere, making it easier to recover data if the school itself is inaccessible.

Finally, schools are also implementing more comprehensive disaster recovery plans. These plans include not just data backup, but also plans for restoring critical systems and infrastructure, such as servers and networks. Disaster recovery plans also include testing and validation to ensure they will work as intended in the event of an actual disaster.

The changes in data backup and disaster recovery strategies in the era of digital transformation apply to smaller school districts as well. In fact, these changes may be even more important for smaller districts, which may have limited resources to deal with the fallout from a disaster.

Many smaller school districts don't have a real data backup and disaster recovery plan. Of course, every small district IT director will say they have backups, but real backups are multi-tiered, scheduled and tested (this is one of the things rarely done with backups).

Smaller school districts may have fewer staff members to handle data backup and disaster recovery, making it even more critical to have efficient and reliable solutions in place. Cloud-based backup solutions, for example, can be particularly useful for smaller districts, as they can provide an affordable and scalable option for backing up data.

Smaller districts may also be more vulnerable to disasters, as they may not have the same level of redundancy in their systems as larger districts. As a result, disaster recovery plans are critical for smaller districts to ensure they can recover quickly in the event of a disaster.

Digital Transformation & Student Computing

Although almost all schools have adopted a platform for student computing, especially after COVID-19, today, more than ever, capable and well managed student devices such as laptops, tablets, and smartphones, are crucial tools in supporting digital transformation in schools.

More than just access to the email, the LMS and productivity applications, they allow students to engage in interactive and collaborative learning, access educational apps and software, and participate in online classes and discussions. Thus, the word "capable" becomes more relevant.

The Virtual Desktop

Virtual desktops can play a crucial role in supporting digital transformation in schools. By providing a virtualized desktop environment, students and teachers can access their applications and data from anywhere, on any device. This flexibility makes it easier for students to learn from home or on the go, without being limited by the hardware available to them. Virtual desktops also simplify software management and updates, as updates can be applied to a central image rather than being installed on individual machines. This reduces the workload for IT staff and ensures that all users are accessing the latest version of software. Additionally, virtual desktops provide a more secure environment, as all data is stored centrally and can be easily backed up and secured. Overall, virtual desktops offer schools a more efficient and flexible way to provide students and teachers with access to their applications and data, supporting the digital transformation of the education sector.

There are several large-scale examples of Virtual Desktop Infrastructure (VDI) deployments in schools. One example is the Los Angeles Unified School District (LAUSD), which implemented VDI in 2013 to provide access to digital resources for its 640,000 students and 30,000 teachers. The VDI deployment included over 35,000 virtual desktops, allowing students and teachers to access educational resources from any device with an internet connection.

Another example is the New York City Department of Education, which implemented VDI to provide remote access to applications and data for its 1.1 million students and over 135,000 staff members. The VDI deployment allowed students and staff to access educational resources from home, providing a more flexible and accessible learning environment. These large-scale VDI deployments demonstrate the potential benefits of virtual desktops in supporting digital transformation in schools, including increased access to resources, greater flexibility, and improved security.

What about Chromebooks?

Chromebooks are not typically considered virtual desktops in the traditional sense. While they do provide a virtualized environment, they are not typically deployed using virtual desktop infrastructure (VDI) solutions. Instead, Chromebooks are designed to run applications and store data in the cloud, providing a more lightweight and cost-effective alternative to traditional desktops or laptops.

While Chromebooks do offer some of the benefits of virtual desktops, such as centralized management and remote access to applications and data, they are not typically used in the same way as VDI solutions. Nonetheless, Chromebooks have become a popular choice for schools due to their affordability, ease of use, and ability to support digital transformation initiatives.

iPads and Tablets

iPads and tablets can be good platforms for student computing, depending on the specific educational goals and needs of the students and teachers. Again, ask the question, how will they be used? iPads and Android-based tablet computers can be very functional devices, particularly for younger students or for specific educational activities that require portability, interactivity, or personalization. However, their limitations and potential distractions need to be carefully considered and managed by teachers and school administrators.

Here are some of the advantages and disadvantages of using iPads and tablets in the classroom:

Advantages

Portability: iPads and tablets are lightweight and portable, making them easy for students to carry around and use in different locations or situations.

Touchscreen Interface: The touchscreen interface is intuitive and user-friendly, making it easy for young students to navigate and use.

Interactive Learning: iPads and tablets can support interactive learning through educational apps and multimedia content, providing students with a more engaging and hands-on learning experience.

Personalization: iPads and tablets can be customized to meet the individual learning needs and preferences of students, providing a more personalized learning experience.

Digital Access: iPads and tablets provide access to a wealth of digital resources, such as eBooks, online learning platforms, and educational videos.

Disadvantages

Limited Functionality: iPads and tablets have limited processing power and storage capacity compared to laptops and desktop computers, which can limit their functionality for more demanding applications.

Software Limitations: Some educational software may not be available or optimized for iPads and tablets, which can limit their use in certain subjects or learning activities.

Fragility: iPads and tablets can be fragile and prone to damage if dropped or mishandled, which can result in costly repairs or replacements.

Cost: iPads and tablets can be more expensive than traditional desktop computers or laptops, which can be a barrier for schools with limited budgets.

Distraction: The portability and interactive nature of iPads and tablets can also be a source of distraction for students, particularly if they are not used in a controlled and supervised manner.

IOS or Android?

Whether iPads or Android tablets are better for student computing depends on the specific needs and goals of the educational environment. Both types of devices have their advantages and disadvantages, so it is important to consider the following factors when choosing between them. Also, both platforms have a somewhat cult following and detractors.

Try not to get caught up in these battles, they're not worth the heartache. There is one major factor in this decision—the more the district and IT department are welcoming of Apple products (iPads, MacBooks, and iMacs), the better the platforms integrate together. But let it also be stated, the Windows PC computing world does not welcome Apple devices into the enterprise. If anything, Windows-based vendors make integration of MacOS devices decidedly less inviting than native Windows PC and Android OS.

Cost

Android tablets are generally less expensive than iPads, which may make them a more affordable option for schools with limited budgets.

Compatibility

If the school is already using other Apple devices or software, iPads may be a better choice for compatibility and ease of use. However, if the school uses Google's suite of apps, Android tablets may be a better choice.

App Selection

iPads have a larger selection of educational apps available in the App Store, but Android tablets have access to Google Play, which also has many educational apps.

Customization

Android tablets offer more customization options, which can be beneficial for tailoring the device to meet the individual needs of students and teachers.

Security

Apple's strict control over the App Store makes it more difficult for malicious software to make its way onto iPads. However, Android has been known to be more vulnerable to security breaches.

User Interface

iPads are known for their intuitive user interface, while Android tablets offer more customization options but can be less intuitive for some users.

Managing Android and Windows devices in a Windows enterprise can be different from managing iPads due to differences in hardware, operating systems, and management tools. Here are some factors to consider:

iPad & Android Management

Management Tools

While Microsoft provides tools to manage both Windows and Android devices through Microsoft Endpoint Manager, managing iPads in a Windows environment requires additional software, such as Apple's Mobile Device Management (MDM) solution. This can add complexity to device management and require additional expertise.

Compatibility

Windows devices are designed to work seamlessly with other Microsoft products and services, while iPads are designed to work with Apple's ecosystem. This can make it more difficult to integrate iPads into a Windows environment and can require additional configuration and software.

Device Settings & Features

Android and Windows devices offer more flexibility in terms of device settings and features, while iPads have a more limited set of options. This can make it easier to customize Android and Windows devices to meet specific enterprise needs.

Training & Expertise

Managing iPads in a Windows enterprise may require additional training and expertise in Apple's ecosystem and MDM solutions, while managing Android and Windows devices may require expertise in those respective ecosystems.

Ultimately, the decision of whether to use iPads or Android tablets for student computing will depend on the specific needs and goals of the educational environment. It is important to carefully consider the advantages and disadvantages of each platform before making a decision.

BYOD

Out of all these student computing options, there is one that in some ways, has already been implemented, whether you've thought about it or not. Schools have either elected to allow students to connect their personal devices to the WIFI or they haven't. But that doesn't stop the typical SmartPhone. We know they have their own 5G network that the school cannot control—and doesn't pay for.

We've already discussed how BYOD can be a security concern and may warrant its own policies and procedures. It would be naive not to consider

BYOD devices within the scope of your school's digital transformation because it is already there, and already being used to some extent, either with the school's blessing, or not.

BYOD can be a component of an overall digital transformation strategy for schools. BYOD allows students to use their personal devices, such as laptops, tablets, and smartphones, to access educational resources and participate in online learning.

One advantage of BYOD is that it can help schools to reduce the cost of providing computing devices for students, as students bring their own devices to use in the classroom. This can free up resources to invest in other areas of digital transformation, such as training for teachers, infrastructure improvements, and the adoption of new digital tools and platforms.

In more middle-class and affluent areas, the device being provided by the schools is less powerful than the students' own devices—SmartPhone and Laptop at a minimum.

In addition, BYOD can promote greater flexibility and customization in learning experiences since students can use devices they are familiar with, and teachers can tailor instruction to the devices and software available to them. This can promote greater student engagement and participation in learning activities.

However, implementing BYOD requires careful planning and consideration of security and privacy concerns as we've already discussed. Schools must have policies and procedures in place to ensure that students' personal devices are secure and do not pose a risk to the school's network or data. They must also ensure that student privacy is protected and that sensitive data is not accessed or shared inappropriately.

CHAPTER SIX

A Digital Transformation Process

A quick review of the digital transformation process (or one of them) is pretty straight-forward. They comprise the obvious steps of defining an end result as a goal, understanding the gap, and developing a plan, such as this methodology:

Step 1: Secure initial executive buy in support
Step 2: Asses your current digital capabilities
Step 3: Set specific goals and objectives
Step 4: Develop a roadmap
Step 5: Implement changes incrementally
Step 6: Invest in training and development
Step 7: Monitor and evaluate
Step 8: Continuously iterate and innovate

This process looks good because it includes some external factors such as securing buy-in and investing in training. They are items that if not secured can ensure that a project never gets off the ground, and if it does, could hinder or deny success over a time frame.

The reality is each step could be very complicated, or require additional specialization or skills. Step 4: develop a roadmap, is likely a minimum of a 6–12 month implementation plan so these steps cannot be considered insignificant.

Other obstacles might exist including non-technical obstacles. Let's get directly into what it might look like to undertake this endeavor in a school district.

CHAPTER SIX

THE DIRECTED TRANSFORMATION PROCESS IN EDUCATION

As we begin this discussion, we must start with examples within your organization. It is important to "test" the likelihood of success for each task as it becomes part of the plan. For instance, part of your Step 1 might include hiring a consultant with digital transformation expertise in school districts of similar size. Then if you go to your manager and he says "no," your digital transformation project just sunk.

As we step through this process, we'll have examples where we'll see that we've already made a significant move in digital transformation. Innumerable small, and many major, examples of how technology has impacted our lives and continues to become more and more efficient and effective.

The relevant discipline necessary to embark on this digital transformation is to start with small, defined achievable goals and objectives and achieve them. Then take on the bigger initiatives once you've established a track record. If you start thinking large-scale initially, you'll encounter many more obstacles, not the least of which will be organizational.

In one example, the IT director of a district proposed to develop a software application that rendered a data processing clerk's job obsolete. However, once the software was in production, the IT director was not able to redeploy or terminate the employee.

Since the objective of the project was to automate a manual process, the project would be considered successful, however, if the employee is not redeployed effectively, they might become a victim of the project's success. No guarantees.

Step 1 - Secure Executive Buy-in and Support

Step 1 is to gain the support of school leadership. Communicate the value and benefits of the digital transformation and ensure that leadership is aligned with the goals and objectives.

It should be noted that an attempt to initiate comprehensive transformation in any organization must have executive sponsorship. No one person, except for the most senior in an organization's leadership can credibly say, "we're going to digitally transform this organization."

Think about the inference, implications, and impacts of this type of assertion. For any single person within an organization to propose to transform it, necessarily infers it has flaws, or at the very least the processes are out-of-date, and at the very worst, obsolete. In some cases, this inference might point to a person or process deeply ingrained in the organization. So even making this assertion can be risky.

But that is not to say that only those in leadership can call for transformation, or more diplomatically, improvement, but if this recognition and call to action is starting at the grass roots of the organization, then it will need to gain mindshare and support by leadership before garnering resources and sanction. Which means it will need to be more than just a complaint or an idea, it will need to be presented as an opportunity. We'll discuss more about developing the opportunity.

The implication of this digital transformation assertion is that the current process can be improved, and a particular person's job might be directly impacted. For example, if your current job is to compile data from demographers, student information, and performance, and someone comes along and automates the process, your job may have been eliminated through digital transformation.

But it is also reasonable to assert that if this process is faster and more accurate, its objective is achieved. Then the organizational impact should be recognized in the best way possible. That is the diplomatic way of saying that unless you redeploy or lay that person off, your department will not benefit from the potential cost savings of lowering the FTE count.

Inferences, implications, and impacts can all play important roles in shaping and affecting digital transformation. Here's how each of these concepts can affect digital transformation:

Inferences are conclusions drawn from available evidence or data. In the context of digital transformation, inferences can help organizations to identify patterns and trends in data that can inform their transformation strategies. For example, a school might analyze data on student interest in a certain new course offerings, to infer what types of courses are most in demand. These inferences can then guide the organization's digital transformation efforts.

For example, if while undergoing an automation project, the project implies that the current process is obsolete or flawed, which in turn might cause employees to infer their jobs will be eliminated. This inference is dangerous if not managed correctly by leadership and those empowered to drive the transformation process.

Implications are the consequences or effects that follow from a particular action or decision. In the context of digital transformation, implications can refer to the potential impacts that new technologies or processes may have on the organization and its stakeholders. For example, the implementation of new digital technologies may have implications for the organization's workforce, requiring new skills or training. Understanding these implications is important for managing the risks and opportunities associated with digital transformation.

Impacts refer to the actual effects that a particular action or decision has on the organization and its stakeholders. In the context of digital transformation, impacts can be positive or negative, depending on how effectively the transformation is managed. For example, digital transformation may lead to increased efficiency and cost savings, but it may also lead to job loss or decreased customer satisfaction if not implemented properly. Understanding the impacts of digital transformation is important for evaluating its success and making adjustments as needed.

Inferences, implications, and impacts all play important roles in shaping and affecting digital transformation. By understanding these concepts, mitigating potential obstructions and liabilities, and incorporating them into their strategies, organizations can more effectively manage the risks and opportunities associated with digital transformation.

Step 2 - Assess Your Current Digital Capabilities

Step 2 is to evaluate your school's existing technology infrastructure, software and hardware, and determine what gaps exist between where you are right now and where you need to be—the end goal. The definition of this step implies the existence of some sort of standard technology infrastructure and suite that supports the end goal. How can we know this when we haven't defined the end goal yet?

In strategic planning we call this the baseline—our starting point. This is the first step for any individual within a school or district to take toward digital transformation. The first question you might ask is who has the capability to perform this assessment? In fact, you might realize that no one particular person currently in your organization has the background or experience to do this assessment.

Who has the technical background, the instructional background and the understanding of the vision to move the organization toward digital transformation? You might need different subject matter experts in various disciplines and fields to perform these assessments. So who can and will be the person to initiate this effort?

Well, since you're reading this book, that person is you. You either have to take it upon yourself to proclaim that you can perform this process, or that you can engage resources who can. You have to take it upon yourself to help others see the need for digital transformation, and in order to do that you have to be able to envision the potential of digital transformation.

Let's look at two examples, an incidental digital transformation and a directed digital transformation. Recall directed in this context means planned versus incidental.

Incidental Digital Transformation

The most simple example of an incidental digital transformation is when your department started using a new software application that is cloud-based. Whether it is digital streaming or software-as-a-service, that move was an incidental digital transformation. So was it beneficial? Did it make processes more streamlined or take less time or fewer resources?

An example of incidental digital transformation in education is the widespread adoption of video conferencing tools during the COVID-19 pandemic. Schools that had previously relied on traditional classroom-based instruction were forced to rapidly adapt to remote learning environments, and many turned to video conferencing tools such as Zoom or Microsoft Teams to facilitate live virtual instruction and collaboration.

There really wasn't much planning at all. Many of these tools were already in production and some widely used. It's just that widely used is still miles away from 100% use. But the technology held up. What was more questionable was the teachers and their adaptability and inherent technology aptitude.

While this shift to virtual learning was initially driven by necessity rather than strategic planning, it has had a profound impact on the way that education is delivered and has led to many incidental digital transformations. For example, teachers have had to learn new skills and techniques for delivering instruction via video conferencing, students have had to adapt to new modes of learning and collaboration, and schools have had to develop new policies and procedures for ensuring student engagement, participation, and accountability in virtual environments.

We've had to learn to use the calendar and connect using the correct tool (Zoom, Teams, Meets or WebEx? And what happened to Skype?).

There is no doubt that for most this was not an easy transition. Teachers and students were given devices and connectivity to the Internet but what then. Teachers (and students) who had been moving toward online curriculum were thrust into the realm, but those less prepared struggled with technical issues and missed opportunities.

Thus is the story of incidental digital transformation. You might call it hit or miss. We've neglected to think through all the implications and impacts. Thus is the case for Directed Digital Transformation.

Directed Digital Transformation

Directed digital transformation is exemplified by the adoption of a Learning Management System (LMS). For maximum benefit, a school must commit to the features and functions of a LMS system. But once it does, and follows through with the professional development, AND the teachers and students all assimilate the workflow and collaboration functions, this is the ultimate example of taking a formerly part digital and part manual process (the act of writing a paper on a computer, then printing it for submission is a fundamental digital process, but then printing it for submission is a manual process).

The learning management system is a digital platform that allows teachers to organize and deliver course materials, manage student progress and performance, and facilitate communication and collaboration among students and teachers. The more teachers and their students assimilate the features and workflows defined by the LMS, the more benefit they derive, as well the school as a whole.

The adoption of an LMS is a directed digital transformation because it involves a deliberate effort to introduce new technologies and tools into the educational environment with the specific goal of improving teaching and learning outcomes. This might involve a comprehensive planning process that considers the needs and preferences of teachers, students, and other stakeholders, as well as the resources and infrastructure required to support the implementation of the LMS. We'll take a deep dive into the LMS later.

Digital transformation initiatives in education entities, must be a sanctioned undertaking by leadership, or it might be a determination by the Chief Technology Officer, but it won't happen on its own (unless it's incidental—this has already been happening), and you won't expect your staff-level employees to have the ability or the time to perform this assessment without some help and guidance.

So what this means is—true digital transformation must be envisioned, defined, and resourced, like any major initiative within the school.

Next—oh yeah, we're still in Step 2 - Assess your school's digital capabilities. What are the digital capabilities to be assessed?

Consider factors such as internet connectivity, access to devices, and software applications. It will quickly become obvious that these digital capabilities exist in both the instructional and administrative side of the operations and will also include vendors, and service providers.

Which also means, that's right, sales people. Sorry to tell you that your digital transformation initiative might get hijacked by some vendors and manufacturers and their products. Don't let it happen. Be sure to manage your vendors, not the reverse.

In step two, schools should assess their current digital capabilities in several areas to determine their current level of technological readiness.

Infrastructure and Connectivity

Assess the school's network infrastructure and internet connectivity to ensure that they can support digital learning tools and devices at a large scale.

Luckily, most schools and districts have been investing in these for many years and should be able to provide access to resources and necessary bandwidth to support the user base.

You might leverage your IT vendor to determine if your school LANs, district WAN, ISP services, firewalls and security are up to snuff. Your IT department should be able to provide bandwidth utilization reports from their equipment and your service providers to make this determination.

Ultimately you don't need to worry about speeds and feeds. The question is, is it working? Is it responsive? Is it reliable? If the answer to these questions is not an unqualified yes, then a professional should be brought in to determine a strategy for technology infrastructure upgrades. Because guess what? If it's not working this year, it won't get better next year without a significant upgrade.

Don't let this assessment kill your initiative. Sometimes a proof of concept can become the justification for the upgrade.

This assessment of infrastructure and connectivity can be summed up with these items:

- Devices—does everyone have one?
- WIFI—is it everywhere?
- Infrastructure—All the necessary WANs, LANs, services, and security to provide access to all users.

Devices and Software

Evaluate the school's existing devices and software applications to determine if they are up-to-date and can meet the needs of teachers and students. It is of the utmost importance to recognize that devices and software have a life cycle, and will become obsolete. So investment in student devices and management suites becomes part of an annual technology refresh budget.

It's really as simple as this example of a school district with 10,000 students and devices with a four-year lifecycle. After initial purchases of devices, the school purchases 25% of enrollment plus some spares each year for new 2nd, 6th and 9th grade students. This device should last four years. Devices can be salvaged and some kept as spares as they age out.

By now, your school or district has come down in one or both of the following cloud services, Microsoft or Google. This move was a significant digital transformation—pat yourself on the back.

These platforms render the software services question moot. As a student or staff of a school or district, you have access to these platforms and there is no reason that significant digital transformation shouldn't already be happening subject to what's currently available.

Learning Management Systems

Learning management systems (LMS) are online platforms that allow educators to deliver, manage and track learning activities, resources and assessments. They play a significant role in supporting digital transformation in schools in the following ways:

LMS provides a centralized platform for managing educational materials and student information, including grades, attendance, and progress. Teachers can upload and organize content and assignments, and students can access them from any location with an internet connection.

LMS platforms allow teachers to create personalized learning paths for students based on their individual needs, interests, and learning styles. This helps to enhance student engagement and motivation, leading to better learning outcomes.

LMS platforms enable collaboration among teachers, students, and parents, creating a more interactive learning experience. Students can participate in group discussions, share resources, and collaborate on projects.

LMS platforms provide a variety of assessment and feedback tools, such as quizzes, surveys, and peer assessments. Teachers can easily monitor student progress and provide feedback on their work.

LMS platforms generate data and analytics that can be used to track student progress and identify areas where students need additional support. This data can also be used to make informed decisions about instructional design and teaching strategies.

Learning management systems support digital transformation in schools by providing a centralized platform for managing educational materials, enabling personalized learning, fostering collaboration, providing assessment and feedback tools, and generating data and analytics. We already made a convincing case for digital transformation through adoption and assimilation of an LMS. Now assess your school's learning management system (LMS) and how it's used by the user-base to determine if it is effective and user-friendly for both teachers and students.

Think of this scenario, when one teacher is still requiring printed assignments. Or worse yet, when the students are using the features and the teacher doesn't know about it. Like using the message boards while the teacher is unaware, or not knowing how to disable them. This can lead to abuse and cyberbullying. Another scenario is where the teacher still prefers homework to be printed and handed in, even though the LMS has a more robust facility to handle multiple homework projects being submitted by hundreds of students.

Once implemented, an LMS can have a profound impact on the teaching and learning experience. Teachers can use the platform to deliver course content and assignments, to track student progress and performance, and to provide personalized feedback and support. Students can use the platform to access course materials, collaborate with peers, and engage with teachers in real-time.

So the LMS becomes the next level of digital transformation by eliminating the printing and submission process, by using the LMS for submission and never having to print the document. But consider the plethora of additional features gained using the LMS. Features that were either manual and non-standardized, and are now centrally available to all via the LMS include:

- Schedule of homework due dates
- Online access to learning resources via LMS and Internet
- Automated timestamping and verification of the submission
- Iterative review and re-submission process
- Message boards and collaboration activities
- Validation and plagiarism checking.

These base-level LMS features and functions provide a dramatic improvement over legacy processes. Learning management systems (LMS) offer a range of advanced features that can enhance the teaching and learning experience, but they are often underutilized by both teachers and students.

One advanced feature is the ability to create personalized learning paths for students based on their individual strengths and weaknesses. With this feature, teachers can provide customized content and activities for each student, which can improve engagement and help students reach their full potential.

Another is the ability to track student progress in real-time, providing teachers with insights into how well students are understanding the material. By monitoring student progress, teachers can identify areas where students may need additional support or intervention and adjust their teaching strategies accordingly.

LMS also often offer advanced assessment and grading features, such as the ability to create and administer complex assessments, and automatic grading. This can save teachers time and allow them to focus on providing personalized feedback and support to their students.

Collaboration and communication tools are advanced features that are often underutilized in LMS. Teachers and students can use these tools to collaborate on projects and assignments, provide feedback to one another, and engage in discussions outside of the classroom. These features can foster a sense of community and provide opportunities for students to practice important skills, such as teamwork and communication.

But implementation of an LMS can also be a blind offering, with leadership adopting an LMS because "every other district is doing it." Fortunately, even if this is the impetus, the benefit will impact all those who assimilate it.

Data Management and Privacy

Evaluate the school's data management practices to ensure that they are in compliance with data privacy laws and regulations. Sometimes data becomes available without those understanding the rules and regulation regarding student data and privacy. Data that wasn't shared electronically before is suddenly online and available to the simple computer hacker before you said, "the new system is up and running."

Data management and privacy are important considerations for schools that collect and use student data, which is all schools. Schools need to ensure that they comply with privacy laws and regulations, such as the Family Educational Rights and Privacy Act (FERPA), which protect the privacy of student education records. This means that schools must obtain consent from parents or eligible students before disclosing personally identifiable information (PII) about a student, and must have policies and procedures in place to safeguard student data.

In addition to complying with privacy laws, schools should also implement best practices for data management to ensure that student data is accurate, secure, and only accessible by authorized persons. Schools should also include student data in the data backup and disaster recovery plans to ensure that student data is not lost in the event of a system failure or other disaster. Lucky for you, that is someone's specific job over in IT and the answer should be, "of course everything is backed up."

Effective data management and privacy practices are essential for schools in the process of digital transformation to protect student data and ensure that it is used ethically and responsibly. By implementing appropriate policies and procedures, schools can safeguard student privacy and ensure that student data is used only for authorized purposes.

Equity & Access

Equity and access are critical considerations in any directed digital transformation in education. While the adoption of new digital technologies and tools has the potential to enhance teaching and learning outcomes, it is important to ensure that all students have equal access to these resources and that they do not exacerbate existing inequalities in the educational system.

One way to ensure equity and access is to consider the needs and preferences of all students when selecting and implementing digital tools and technologies. This might involve consulting with teachers, students, and other stakeholders to identify the resources and infrastructure required to support the implementation of new technologies and to ensure that they are accessible to all students, regardless of their background or socioeconomic status.

It is also important to provide training and support to teachers and students to ensure that they are able to effectively use and leverage these new technologies in their learning and teaching environments. This might involve providing ongoing professional development opportunities for teachers and technical support for students, as well as developing policies and procedures to ensure that all students are able to access and utilize these resources in a fair and equitable manner.

Professional Development

Assess the professional development opportunities available to teachers to determine if they are sufficient for them to integrate technology effectively into their teaching.

Ask this question. What percent of the teachers are using the LMS effectively? The percentage of students utilizing the LMS is significantly dependent on their teacher's utilization of the services provided in the LMS.

If this number is below 50 percent, then some generalized training should be offered. If as high as 70 percent, then the teacher mentors can work with those not maximizing the features of the LMS.

It might state that WIFI coverage throughout most schools sites is adequate to support each student with a device on the WIFI network (or not). It should state if the district's Internet connectivity will support online learning for all students simultaneously. It should state if all students have access to devices and if teachers' classrooms have been outfitted with a standard suite of technology tools. Finally it should state if all software suites to support productivity and LMS functionality are fully operational and teachers are trained.

The outcome of Step 2 - Assess Your Digital Capabilities should be a report and a rough order magnitude (ROM) budget. The report should detail a baseline for your school's digital capabilities against a background of what we should have and what we should be.

The ROM should be developed to project costs to improve and achieve this baseline performance level in order to move toward digital transformation at each site and support online learning in future years. It's logical to ask at this point what we do with this "digital capabilities assessment?" Obviously, the leadership team that sanctioned this Step 2 of your digital transformation initiative should receive this report, and respond with advice of their backing and commitment along with the direction to move to Step 3.

Step 3 - Set Specific Goals and Objectives

Step 3 - Define the outcomes you hope to achieve with your digital transformation, such as improving student engagement, enhancing teaching and learning, and increasing operational efficiency.

Although the statement at the beginning of Step 2 is well stated, the goals are not objective enough. Let's take another shot at what a description of specific goals and objectives might be.

Step 3, define the outcomes you hope to achieve with your digital transformation, such as improving student engagement from current levels to full utilization, enhancing teaching and learning through professional development and optimization of existing tools and resources, and increasing operational efficiency by eliminating manual, repetitive and / or redundant processes.

These might be outcomes from one or separate endeavors. The point is that objectives should be objective. They should be provable if not measurable.

Improving Student Engagement

Improving student engagement by measuring utilization of the LMS and productivity suite is a good baseline. But how would we measure utilization? The first and easiest method would be to ask each teacher about their utilization of the specific features of the LMS. If teacher utilization is low, then it could be assumed that student utilization follows. That's not to say that student utilization can't be higher than teacher utilization, but if some teachers aren't optimizing the LMS functionality, they should be trained and encouraged to do so.

Learning management systems (LMS) can improve student engagement in several ways:

LMS platforms become the glue for class and lesson content, resources, queries and prompts, and work submission. Once effectively trained, teachers and students are able to facilitate all methods and phases of lesson plan delivery and collaboration to support synchronous interactions as well as asynchronous so all learning resources and video conferences are available for later viewing.

Once students understand that all their interactions and information required to be successful are encompassed by the LMS, each student will learn to maximize the LMS to their greatest advantage.

The LMS allows teachers to create personalized learning paths for students based on their individual needs, interests, and learning styles.

The LMS enables collaboration among teachers, students, and parents, creating a more global learning experience. Students can participate in group discussions, share resources, and collaborate on projects, with entities and individuals outside the academic sphere which helps to foster a greater sense of community and global engagement.

LMS platforms provide immediate feedback on student performance, which helps to keep students and teachers engaged with each other. Teachers can use feedback tools to provide constructive criticism and praise, both in feedback as well as chat and direct messaging available on the LMS..

The LMS can be accessed from any location with an internet connection, making it possible for students to learn at their own pace and on their own time with their own devices. This flexibility can help to keep students informed and engaged, especially if they have busy schedules or have opportunities to learn outside of the classroom.

Enhancing Teaching & Learning

The author's previous books about Tier 4 Curriculum provide a deep dive and prescription to implement T4c at your school. The point is most related to two platforms, the LMS and the productivity suite (Google Apps for Education or MS Office).

Once again, a survey of teachers' utilization of the productivity suite can set the baseline for improvement. Measure your teachers' utilization of word processor, spreadsheet and slide presentation functions and features within your productivity suite.

As the second tier, a survey of students' utilization of the productivity suite can provide a secondary baseline for improvement. The issue in this example however is what type of training and enhanced learning can be offered to students?

Or alternately forget the surveys and go straight to training. Keeping in mind that training is multi-tiered. Starting at the base-level there's the device operating system and access to digital resources via apps or web browsers.

Then there's access to resources, working with credentials and passwords (MFA, SSO) and other security processes and practices.

Make these trainings for teachers regularly and provide them via online videos that all can access via the LMS training portal.

Increasing Operational Efficiency

Define the outcomes you hope to achieve with your digital transformation, like increasing operational efficiency by eliminating manual, repetitive and / or redundant processes. This is a nice little exercise that each team member can do on their own as a starting point. For this assessment determine if there are manual, repetitive and / or redundant processes in your daily operations and then overlay that inquiry on your department and operational teams.

The idea is that all manual tasks are eliminated through the process of optimizing existing systems and technologies. Identify productivity features and functions not well utilized within your department. Look for the use of manual or semi-manual processes being used by other team members.

You might be asking yourself, who can undertake this task? You can't just go around asking people what they do minute-by-minute without, 1) getting in their way and decreasing their productivity, 2) making them feel like they are being audited or monitored. That's likely not your role.

You might need approval from leadership to do an Operational Efficiency assessment. Start via an email survey for staff soliciting suggestions for operational efficiency and improvement. By engaging with their sensibilities and providing an opportunity to have an impact on their workflows.

For example, if a team member is using Excel or Google spreadsheet, that process can immediately be questioned. What are they using the spreadsheet for?

And can the process be automated using a database or productivity-based application. Can it be made to be more accurate and faster? Is this something they are doing regularly? Where is the data coming from and going to? Regarding this example, the goal would be to eliminate this manual process with an automated one, with greater accuracy and reliability.

Another way of increasing operational efficiency is to train all the users in a department in the preferred way of using each productivity application within the designated suite. Most users of applications like Excel or Google Sheets understand and utilize less than 10 percent of the application's capabilities. How many times have seen someone using Excel when Word tables would be more effective, or worse, making calculations on a handheld calculator and entering them in cells in an excel sheet?

Step 4 - Develop a Roadmap

Create a plan for how to achieve your digital transformation objectives. Identify the steps, timelines, resources, and stakeholders needed to carry out the plan, such as teachers, students, parents, and administrators.

Now that you've got executive buy-in, an understanding of current utilization of tools, and some baselines for improvement, you can begin to develop plans for digital transformation. This roadmap might be a long range strategy that includes small incremental improvements and major operational shifts, or it might be a sequence of smaller digital transformation initiatives.

Like any plan, the roadmap should include the objectives, the resources, the tactical plans, resource plans and timelines.

Digital transformation might require a diverse team of skilled professionals, including instructional designers, IT professionals, curriculum developers, and data analysts. Building a strong team with the right mix of skills and expertise is essential to the success of a digital transformation initiative.

This roadmap also becomes a progress measurement tool over time. By locking in the scheduled due dates and actions, use the same tools to note the actual installation and operational dates.

This sample timeline is a conceptually simple three phase digital transformation plan.

> Phase 1 is to train staff in the correct and preferred use of the Office suite, including how particular processes and forms should look as a standard for the department. This is on top of their requisite technology fundamental cybersecurity training.

> Phase 2 is to upgrade from a legacy procurement application the department has been using for the past decade to a newer, cloud-based application that has many more options and features that will enhance the department's procurement and contracts processes. This newer application also has integration with the school districts' county and state report requirements.

> Phase 3 of this plan is for the department to work with the IT development team to automate a legacy forms processing and archival system. By developing a customized database application that addresses a legacy process that is mostly manual, the department intends to save hours of manual processing hours and human errors that are most common.

> Phase 3 might include training for IT staff to customize, operate and support the new platform.

Step 5 - Implement Changes Incrementally

Rather than attempting to implement digital transformation changes at once, roll out changes incrementally. Start with a small pilot program to test new technology solutions, and expand as you gain feedback and insights. Small

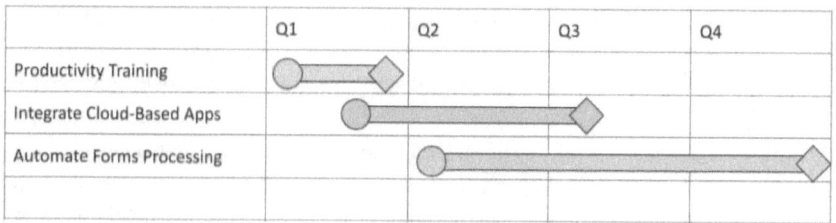

Figure 6.1   Timeline

successes will lead to larger ones. But starting out too big invites obstacles and increases risks. Many that are unforeseen, for obvious reasons.

This can be seen in the timeline in step 4. Each initiative is begun on its own. Not until progress has begun on the first initiative can the second start. Obviously, if the same resources are to execute on the plan, the likelihood is that they would be mostly sequential. One project waiting for the previous project to be completed.

But the more important point is that digital transformation takes time. It takes time for people to adjust from legacy processes. It takes time for them to work these changes into their routines. Be patient but stay on the path. It may take two-to-three years to fully implement an LMS system.

Give users time to assimilate the new processes, but don't relent. Don't give in to requests to go back to the old way. It should be thought of as a one-way transformation for the better.

Implementing digital transformations incrementally can offer several benefits to schools. First and foremost, incremental implementation allows schools to manage the risks associated with digital transformations by identifying and addressing potential issues in small, manageable stages. This approach allows schools to make adjustments as needed and avoid costly mistakes that could negatively impact student learning.

Any project manager knows that at every phase of a project, there are challenges and obstacles that weren't anticipated. Smaller scopes have fewer obstacles. This is more manageable in general practice.

An incremental rollout minimizes disruptions to the teaching and learning process, as teachers and students are not required to adapt to major changes all at once. Instead, changes are introduced gradually, allowing for a smoother transition and less disruption to daily routines.

Implementation in phases allows schools to build their capacity for digital transformation over time. By starting with small, manageable changes, schools can build the necessary infrastructure, resources, and expertise needed for larger-scale digital transformations in the future. Also, providing appropriate training at each phase allows the project managers to assess the process and training to be revised and improved over time.

This approach also allows schools to engage stakeholders, including teachers, students, parents, and administrators, in the digital transformation process. By involving stakeholders in the process and addressing their concerns and feedback, schools can build support for the initiative and ensure its success.

Finally, incremental implementation allows schools to demonstrate progress and celebrate successes along the way. This approach can help build momentum and support for the initiative, and can provide motivation for teachers and students to continue exploring new digital tools and technologies.

Step 6 - Invest in Training and Development

In order to close the loop and ensure that teachers and students are equipped with the necessary skills and knowledge to use new digital tools and systems, schools must provide training and development opportunities to not only help them adapt to changes, but to get every penny out of the LMS and accompanying products and services.

One of the most important success factors for any type of training or professional development is that users must be accommodated for their time commitment. Training takes time away from functional operations and normal day-to-day responsibilities.

Be sure the training is appropriate for the role each of your users are undertaking. There's nothing worse than sitting through a training curriculum that isn't relevant to each user's scope and scale of responsibilities, or that isn't provided at the same time as the implementation.

Getting training several months before adoption of such a massive system will only ensure that they'll need more training later. But it should also reinforce the fact that such training must be a periodic endeavor. It would be negligent to think that this type of training is a "one and done" situation.

In addition, incentives or stipends might be warranted to support training activities—then again, there's nothing like coffee, donuts and a free lunch to help in any training or development endeavor.

For students it fits a little better into their curriculum. Teachers should set aside a couple of times to introduce and review the training materials in class. Teachers should be ready to demonstrate the features of the new systems and processes, and demonstrate the benefits.

Teachers must feel comfortable with their new-found expertise, in order to provide the incentive for students to recognize the features and benefits of new technologies—sometimes.

We must also recognize that in this era of technology ubiquity, adults often take on the role of, "if you can figure it out, please show me." Although this is not the preferred model for digital transformation, it can be successful.

Step 7 - Monitor and Evaluate Progress

Continuously monitor your progress towards your digital transformation goals. Use data and analytics to measure the effectiveness of your digital initiatives and adjust your strategy as needed.

It would be great to have metrics and baselines to evince the benefits of a digital transformation, but that will not always be the case. Digital transformation should make processes faster and more reliable, accurate and efficient. If the assimilation of the new processes isn't immediately demonstrative of being more efficient and more effective, then some baselines and metrics are warranted.

A simple stopwatch or elapsed time measurement of a legacy process, as compared to a new digital transformation, should demonstrate these efficiencies. Remember that these won't be apples to apples comparisons. If a process that used to take a full day, now takes less interactive time, but more elapsed time, it still may be more effective. Conversely, some tasks may require such priority as to have a resource dedicated to responding, something that could never be farmed out off premise.

Be sure to set the expectations with leadership that the benefits may not be readily demonstrated in a short term. It is important to note, functional efficiencies and increased accuracy and reliability, and /or lower cost may offer less obvious, but important benefits regardless.

The best way to demonstrate improvement, will be to have a fully documented legacy process, that can then be compared to the new digital transformation process. It would be very easy to demonstrate how training can improve the use and application of new systems over legacy systems.

Ultimately, the users and organization should experience the benefits of more efficient and effective use of technology so it won't have to be proven.

Step 8 - Continuously Iterate and Innovate

Digital transformation is an ongoing process, and schools should continually look for ways to improve and innovate, staying up-to-date with emerging technologies and trends and being willing to make changes as needed.

If we look backward at our own digital transformation over the past years, we'll see that every new technology assimilated into the organization represents a new milestone in digital transformation. From the single computer in the classroom (doing what?) to the teacher's desktop computer, to the one-to-one computer and the individual user-account on the cloud-based LMS, each represents a new level of efficiency and effectiveness not envisioned by the lay-user.

The whole point of this step is that this cycle of constant innovation and automation is inherent, and no effort should be made to impede it. In fact, the more you as an individual within an organization can help to facilitate a digital transformation, the better opportunity for the transformation to benefit each individual and drive innovation from the ground up.

To draw out an example of such impediment, think of any example in your department that requires hardcopy—stuff printed on paper. Why hasn't the need to print something on paper been completely eliminated within the organization?

Yes—I like to read reports off paper sometimes. It's still more portable and disposable. You can mark it up with a red pen. But there should be NO process within your department or organization that requires hardcopy printed material any more.

Of course, this is not absolute. There are still many situations where printed hardcopy is a requirement, despite the increasing use of digital technologies.

Many legal documents, such as contracts, deeds, and wills, require a printed hardcopy with signatures and notarization for validity and authenticity. Medical records are often maintained in hardcopy form due to privacy concerns and regulatory requirements. Printed records are easier to secure and protect against cyberattacks. While digital textbooks and e-learning materials are becoming more common, many students and educators still prefer printed materials for studying and note-taking.

Passports, driver's licenses, and other forms of identification are typically issued in hardcopy form with security features to prevent forgery. Also, printed hardcopy is still essential for preserving and displaying art and photography. High-quality prints offer better color accuracy and durability compared to digital displays.

While digital technologies have replaced many forms of printed materials, printed hardcopy is still a requirement in such situations, particularly when authenticity, privacy, or quality is a concern.

We'll see that almost all of the digital transformation we've personally experienced over the last decade has been delivered via our smartphones, as we discussed early on. And our smartphones will continue to become the mechanism for the near-term except for the corporations and educational organizations.

Where the smartphone reigns in the individual space, the standard computing interface for the corporate user, teacher and student will continue to be an app or browser-based device.

Developing the Opportunity for Directed Digital Transformation

We discussed earlier that the first stage of directed digital transformation is actually getting executive buy-in. You can't go about making changes and impacting individuals and the organization without it. So even before you take that first step of seeking executive buy-in, you must be prepared with a proposal and presentation to address all the possible objections.

Define Your Digital Transformation Objective

In the context of K–12 education, a "digital transformation objective" typically refers to a specific goal or effort related to integrating technology and digital tools into various aspects of teaching and learning.

Digital transformation objectives can vary depending on the specific context and goals of the educational institution or district. For example, a digital transformation objective may include increasing the use of digital tools for student assessment and feedback, providing more opportunities for online or blended learning, or enhancing communication and collaboration between teachers, students, and parents through digital platforms, such as an LMS.

Better yet, many digital transformation initiatives are to address dysfunction or procedural challenges. Anything that involves manual data capture or data entry poses opportunities for human error. Also, moving data from one system to another can prove unreliable. If these processes aren't automated with the appropriate constraints and validation, they too pose opportunities for errors or delays.

Digital transformation objectives often involve the adoption of new technologies, the development of digital literacy skills among teachers and students, and the integration of technology into existing curricula and teaching practices. Most, to all of these "technologies" are software-based, since the hardware is mostly in place.

Gone are the days where companies are inventing lower-cost, dedicated hardware devices for students, such as: voting machines, digital input tablets and handheld scanners. Thank God we've passed that era. Except for science or specialized sporting equipment, pretty much all new technologies are capable of running on PCs, tablets and smartphones. Even $300 Chromebooks are basically almost disposable now.

Every new IoT device a person learns, they are likely adopting in order to become more efficient and effective. Every hint, lifehack, shortcut and app you load is a minor to major digital transformation.

Basically, everyone is undergoing constant digital transformations everyday, but the largest most effective digital transformation initiatives are the ones that disrupt the organization's status quo.

The ultimate goal of digital transformation in K–12 education is to improve learning outcomes and prepare students for success in an increasingly digital world, but we know that digital transformation can have as much, if not more, impact on the administrative side of the house. In fact, we see that the administrative side of a school district is often neglected in digital transformation projects focused on student learning.

However, it can't be denied that making administration more reliable, accurate and efficient also supports student learning.

Give It a Name

In the author's book, *Project Management in the Ed Tech Era*, he provides great detail about project management and the importance of naming projects. Every project must have a name. Without a name, the project cannot take on an identity and characteristic branding of its own.

By having a name, the PM can become responsible for the project and can engage resources and stakeholders on behalf of the project. Without a name, the project cannot be owned and delivered successfully. That is not to say a software can't be selected and implemented without a project name, but no matter, it *will* have a name, even if it's just "Software Upgrade Project."

The name should allude to the instructional or organizational objective of the project or initiative. That's why one-to-one is not a good project name; although it is probably used in about every district, it's widely used not because of its academic goals but because of its trendiness. "One-to-one" is inherently technology focused and doesn't provide any insight or context for the project except that there are devices for each student.

Just as branding is a major factor in marketing and sales, so is branding of the digital transformation project name. What sounds more exciting, "Cloud upgrade" or "Romeo and Juliet Tech"? All this discussion about the name of a project may seem silly, but the reality is, if you can't name your project, is there really a project? In fact, not naming a project is a sure way to diminish the importance of the project or endeavor.

Understand the Scope of Your Digital Transformation Concept

It would be difficult to enumerate the varieties of digital transformation concepts but the important point for this discussion is that if you are spearheading a digital transformation initiative, and preparing to present a proposal to leadership, there must be a clear understanding of scope—the systems, processes, departments and individuals that will be impacted by this transformation.

Nothing could be worse than proposing a major operational change within your organization while those most impacted understand neither the impact or benefit to their departments and workloads.

In fact, if your initiative doesn't clearly illustrate how your digital transformation initiative will positively impact them, those affected might actually line up to diminish and / or sabotage your efforts.

For example, a digital transformation initiative to streamline departmental processes by adopting a new cloud-based service might trigger compatibility issues with current technology systems. A new cloud-based service might require the most recent version of Google Chrome, while some departments are still standardized on Internet Explorer.

Users loading Chrome might cause other services to break, triggering the need for memory or software upgrades. Were these costs projected? What happens if these upgrades cannot be funded?

What might happen if this new cloud-based service actually eliminated the need for some personnel? How might the department be impacted? Would union issues arise? Nothing like getting a union grievance filed because of your digital transformation project.

You might need help understanding the scope of your digital transformation project. In this cloud-based service example, technicians from the IT department might need to be engaged to research the impact of the technical needs.

It's easy to read a marketing brochure that promises all software is backward compatible with your platform but has it been tested? Can you find other schools with the same platforms running the new service? This type of background research is necessary to truly understand the scope of your digital transformation initiative. Remember—systems, processes, departments and individuals.

Develop an Implementation Plan

Sound implementation planning is always the key to project success, and It's not guaranteed. Implementation planning can be exhaustive and detailed to the Nth degree and still fail because of external factors or internal dissension. Alternately, sometimes you just get lucky and everything works and everyone is happy.

But it's still better to have a detailed plan, because the process of developing and documenting a plan will always bear out possible issues and risks.

Here's some important aspects about developing your digital transformation project's implementation plan:

Be sure all your assumptions are valid and true—there's nothing worse than assuming your departmental users are unhappy with a process and that they will welcome your digital transformation. Remember that change can be difficult.

At the same time, that's not to say that the end-users are always right. Just because they don't agree with you doesn't mean that your assumptions are wrong. It might just mean that your efforts aren't addressing their discomfort with current processes.

Plan for training within the scope and timeline of your digital transformation implementation plan. It won't work to implement changes without sufficient training. Not only will end users be confused, but they might cause operational or procedural errors that undermine your proposed "improvement."

Keep a finger on the pulse of the user-base. Make sure your project team understands the concerns of those who might be impacted before they are forced to make the change.

Document and memorialize the new processes and procedures so that they can be spread throughout the organization with positive impact for all. You won't want your new users to spread the operational processes incorrectly—document, train and reinforce.

It's a little disconcerting that some digital transformation processes happen automatically without objection or obstruction. Very few people get new fun technology and don't want to adopt or learn about it. Especially if it makes their job easier and more efficient.

However, the time and training commitment might be onerous. Make sure the preparation and training are supported with time and resources. Never take the position, that they are on their own. Things can and will blow up in days or even minutes.

If you need a treatise on this process, the author has written a whole book on planning educational technology initiatives called, *FAIL TO PLAN, PLAN TO FAIL: How to Create Your School's Education Technology Strategic Plan*—available where books are sold.

Develop a ROM Budget

If you don't know what a Rough Order Magnitude (ROM) budget is or how to create one, pick up the author's book "Fail to Plan, Plan to Fail." It provides a comprehensive yet concise process for developing a ROM budget within the scope and scale of a typical school district technology program.

The ROM must include hard costs such as software licenses, hardware and infrastructure, and training expenses. But it should also include soft costs such as lost productivity or resource time away from tasks during the implementation process.

It is important to identify the various costs associated with the initiative, including hardware, software, training, staffing, and ongoing maintenance and support. It may be helpful to break down costs by phase, such as the initial planning and design phase, the implementation phase, and the ongoing support and maintenance phase. Think of the timeline and break up the ROM budget costs accordingly.

Once the costs have been identified, it is important to estimate the budget required for the initiative. This should involve developing a ROM budget that provides a rough estimate of the total costs, based on the available information and assumptions about the initiative along with some contingency of escalation and inflation.

To develop a ROM budget, it may be helpful to use a range of estimates and assumptions, and to build in contingency funds to account for unforeseen costs or changes in scope. It is also important to consider the potential return on investment (ROI) of the initiative, including the potential cost savings and other benefits that may be realized over time.

It will be important to review the ROM budget with key stakeholders and to seek input and feedback on the various cost estimates and assumptions. This can help ensure that the budget is realistic, feasible, and aligned with the goals and objectives of the digital transformation initiative.

Basically you can't propose any digital transformation initiative without this. It will be the first question asked about your proposal after its initial concept is presented. And if it's not reasonable and affordable relative to the impact you're projecting, forget it. In fact, you may stop developing your proposal once you've created the ROM. There may be so much additional cost or resources required that you decide your digital transformation proposal is not reasonable and cost effective.

For example, suppose you plan on adopting a new LMS platform for your school. This new platform will undoubtedly require licensing fees. However, your district already has a site license for the current LMS. Not only will you be proposing a diversion from the district standard, but the cost of the district standard is already sunk.

In essence, unless your proposed project can realistically offset the sunk costs, resource and training requirements, your proposal won't get off the ground. But if your project will eliminate recurring costs, such as special forms or special services, the new proposed service might present a significant cost savings and leadership might be more receptive.

Present Your Digital Transformation Proposal

Whether your project needs to have an audience with cabinet and board members, or just with your boss, be prepared to address all aspects of your proposal.

Presenting a proposal for digital transformation in a school requires careful planning and preparation to ensure that the proposal is effective and persuasive. There are several important factors to consider when presenting a proposal for digital transformation in a school.

Start at the Beginning

First, it is important to clearly define the goals and objectives of the digital transformation initiative and to align these goals with the needs and priorities of the school community. This may involve conducting a needs assessment to identify the specific challenges and opportunities facing the school, and to develop a clear understanding of how digital technologies can help address these challenges and support student learning.

Talk about the Benefits

Articulate the benefits and potential outcomes of the digital transformation initiative, such as improved student engagement, increased academic achievement, and enhanced teacher collaboration and professional development. It may be helpful to provide specific examples and case studies of other schools or districts that have successfully implemented similar initiatives.

Present a Comprehensive Plan

It is important to develop a comprehensive and realistic plan for the digital transformation initiative, including timelines, budgets, staffing requirements, and a clear plan for measuring and evaluating progress and success. It may be helpful to break down the plan into specific phases or milestones to help manage the implementation process and ensure that the initiative stays on track.

Engage Key Stakeholders

Engage directly with key stakeholders in the digital transformation initiative, including teachers, administrators, students, and parents, and to provide opportunities for feedback and input throughout the planning and implementation process. This can help ensure that the initiative is aligned with the needs and priorities of the school community and can help build support and buy-in for the initiative.

Be Realistic about Cost & Challenges

Finally, it is important to be transparent and open about the ROM costs and challenges associated with the digital transformation initiative and to develop a clear plan for addressing any concerns or objections that may arise. This can help build trust and credibility with stakeholders and can help ensure that the proposal is ultimately successful.

So now you've developed the game plan to take your organization to the next level. You, as the project manager, must carry the project forward. It may take more time, effort and advocacy on your part, and others' to realize the benefit of digital transformation. The thing to remember, and to use as motivation as you move your organization and colleagues toward digital transformation, is that they already assimilate incidental digital transformation almost every day.

CHAPTER SEVEN

Artificial Intelligence in K–12 Education

IT'S ALREADY HERE

AI is already being used in various ways in K–12 education to enhance teaching and learning, provide personalized support to students, and improve educational outcomes, and you didn't even know it.

It is understandable for some teachers to be concerned about the impact of AI on their profession. However, it is important to note that AI is still in its early stages of development, and there are certain aspects of teaching that require human interaction and personalization that are difficult for AI to replicate. For example, the ability to empathize, understand and respond to the unique needs and emotions of each student, and to adapt teaching methods to different learning styles.

Furthermore, the role of a teacher is not limited to imparting knowledge, but also involves instilling values, encouraging critical thinking, and promoting creativity and innovation. These are skills that require human intelligence, experience, and judgment, which AI is not capable of replicating.

Instead of replacing teachers, AI has the potential to enhance their teaching abilities by providing personalized learning experiences, automating administrative tasks, and providing insights into student performance and progress.

While there may be some concerns about the impact of AI on teaching jobs, it is unlikely that AI will replace teachers entirely. Instead, it is more likely that AI will be used to augment and enhance their abilities, making their jobs easier and more effective. But what about the dark side? How much cheating can be accomplished using AI?

With the release of OpenAI's ChatGPT in November of 2022 and Google's Bard, released in March of 2023, users now have a direct vehicle to query and copy results from AI systems. In fact, these AI chatbots are so good, teachers would be hard pressed to determine if the work is original student work, or simply a response to an AI query. Except that the AI response would be grammatically correct all the time.

As the use of AI in education continues to grow, it is becoming increasingly important for school districts to develop policies and guidelines that address its use. These policies should cover areas such as student data privacy, ethical considerations, and the appropriate use of AI tools in teaching and learning.

In addition, policies should also consider issues related to equity and access. AI tools have the potential to improve student learning outcomes and promote greater equity in education, but they also have the potential to exacerbate existing inequities if they are not implemented in an equitable manner. School districts should be mindful of these considerations when developing policies related to AI use in the classroom.

There are some school boards that have implemented policies related to the use of Artificial Intelligence (AI) in the classroom.

The Santa Fe Public Schools in New Mexico has adopted a policy on AI and machine learning that includes guidelines for the ethical use of AI in the classroom, as well as guidelines for protecting student data privacy. The policy also includes provisions for training teachers and staff on the appropriate use of AI tools and for involving parents and students in the decision-making process related to AI use.

The San Francisco Unified School District has also developed a policy on AI that outlines the ethical and responsible use of AI tools in teaching and learning. The policy emphasizes the importance of using AI in a way that is transparent, fair, and equitable, and includes guidelines for protecting student data privacy.

Their policy also prohibits the use of AI in the classroom that could "lead to discrimination, bias, or other negative impacts on students."

The New York City Department of Education (NYCDOE) has a policy that requires that AI systems be used in a way that "is consistent with the NYCDOE's values of equity, diversity, and inclusion." The policy also requires that AI systems be used in a way that "protects the privacy and confidentiality of student data."

Potential Negative Impacts & Challenges

While AI has the potential to enhance and improve education, it also presents certain risks that should be considered. Here are some potential risks that AI could pose to education:

Bias

AI algorithms can inherit biases from their training data, which could result in discrimination against certain groups of students. AI systems can be biased and perpetuate existing inequalities in education. If AI systems are not properly designed and monitored, they could reinforce existing biases in grading, student tracking, and other educational processes. For example, an AI-powered grading system may give lower grades to students with certain ethnicities or genders due to biased training data.

Privacy

The use of AI in education will result in the collection of large amounts of personal data on students, which could be vulnerable to cyber attacks or unauthorized access. It is not currently understood how platforms like ChatGPT and Bard, are dealing with confidential information that has been voluntarily given to them. As long as these platforms can be programmed to understand privacy and what data is considered confidential, there will always be a risk.

Reliance

Over-reliance on AI-powered tools could result in a reduction in critical thinking and creativity among students, as well as a decreased ability to make decisions and solve problems independently. Once introduced into the classroom, there's no telling what might happen to critical thinking skills and collaborative efforts.

It will likely be discovered that similar to drug addiction, some personality types are more susceptible to becoming reliant and even addicted to the abilities of AI platforms, while others might be able to exploit them for some tasks and do other tasks on their own. We are truly on dangerous ground.

Job Displacement

While it is unlikely that AI will replace teachers entirely, there is a risk that it could lead to the displacement of certain jobs in education, such as administrative and support roles.

While AI has the potential to revolutionize education, it is important to carefully consider the potential risks and benefits before implementing AI technologies in the classroom. Education stakeholders must ensure that AI is used ethically, transparently, and in a way that benefits students and teachers alike.

Lack of Personalization

While AI has the potential to personalize learning for each student, it could also lead to a lack of personalization if the technology is not properly designed. AI systems may rely too heavily on standardized algorithms and data points and fail to recognize the unique needs and strengths of individual students.

A lack of personalization can have negative impacts on both students and teachers. When teachers do not tailor their teaching methods to suit individual student needs, some students may struggle to learn.

For example, some students may be visual learners, while others may be auditory learners. If a teacher only uses one teaching method for all students, some students may not be able to understand the material as well as others. This can lead to learning difficulties and a lack of progress in academic performance.

In addition, if students do not feel personally connected to the material they are learning, they may become disengaged and lose interest in the subject. Personalization can help to make learning more meaningful and relevant to each student's interests and abilities. For instance, if a teacher incorporates a student's personal interests into a lesson plan, the student is more likely to be engaged and motivated to learn.

If teachers do not have the resources or support to personalize their teaching methods, they may become overwhelmed and experience burnout. Personalization can help to create a more manageable workload and improve job satisfaction. When teachers are able to tailor their teaching methods to meet individual student needs, they may feel more fulfilled in their role and better equipped to support their students.

The Singularity

In mathematics, a singularity refers to a point in a function or surface where the function or surface is not well-behaved or undefined.

In physics, a singularity refers to a point in space-time where the laws of physics break down or become undefined, such as the center of a black hole.

In technology and futurism, the term "singularity" is often used to refer to a hypothetical moment in the future when artificial intelligence surpasses human intelligence, leading to an exponential increase in technological advancement and a potentially unpredictable future. This is also known as the technological singularity.

There is no widely accepted timeframe for when the technological singularity might occur, and predictions about its arrival are highly speculative.

Some experts predict that it could happen in the next few decades, while others believe that it may not happen for centuries, or may not happen at all.

One of the most well-known predictions came from futurist and computer scientist Ray Kurzweil, who predicted that the singularity would occur by 2045. Kurzweil based his prediction on a combination of Moore's Law (which states that the number of transistors on a microchip doubles roughly every two years) and his own observations about the pace of technological progress.

However, it's important to note that the prediction of the technological singularity is highly controversial, and many experts disagree with Kurzweil's prediction. Some argue that the development of artificial general intelligence (AGI) is much more difficult than anticipated, and that we may not be able to create AGI for decades or even centuries. Others argue that the singularity is unlikely to happen at all, or that it may not have the transformative impact that some predict.

The potential impact of the technological singularity on humanity and the world is a topic of much debate and speculation among experts. Some futurists and researchers argue that the technological singularity could lead to a utopian future of abundance and prosperity, where advanced technologies solve many of the world's problems and enhance human abilities.

However, there are also concerns that the technological singularity could have negative consequences, such as the emergence of powerful and uncontrollable artificial intelligence that could pose an existential threat to humanity. Some experts worry that an advanced AI could act against human interests and goals, or even potentially eliminate humans altogether.

It's important to note that these scenarios are hypothetical and based on uncertain predictions about the future of technology. While the technological singularity is a topic of significant discussion and interest among researchers, it is impossible to say with certainty what its impact will be. As such, it's crucial for scientists and policymakers to continue to monitor and evaluate the development of advanced technologies to minimize the risks and maximize the benefits.

AI Out of Control

Program trading in the stock market and AI share some similarities in terms of their ability to operate autonomously and potentially have unintended consequences.

In program trading, computer algorithms are used to execute large-scale trades in response to market conditions, without the need for human intervention. This can result in rapid and large-scale changes in the stock market, which can have unintended consequences and contribute to market volatility.

Similarly, AI systems can also have unintended consequences. These systems are designed to learn and make decisions based on patterns in data, and can operate autonomously without human intervention. However, if these systems are not properly designed and tested, they can make decisions that are biased or result in unintended consequences.

Both program trading and AI demonstrate the potential risks associated with the use of complex automated systems in high-stakes environments. While these systems can be powerful tools for decision-making and analysis, they must be designed, tested, and monitored carefully to avoid unintended consequences and protect against potential risks.

Emergent Capabilities

Emergent capabilities of AI are abilities that are not explicitly programmed into an AI system, but that emerge as a result of the system's interactions with its environment. These capabilities can be very powerful, and they can often surprise even the engineers who designed the system.

In essence, AI can teach itself. It could take all the writings of the political leaders leading up to the start of World War 1 and develop a definitive event or root cause for what had not been understood or analyzed before. Up through the present day, most historians discuss many social and geo-political factors that brought the tensions to a point where the assassination of Archduke Franz Ferdinand of Austria-Hungary became the trigger for the first World War.

But AI, and its ability to ingest all related (and seemingly unrelated) text about the subject matter may be able to identify factors that no one could imagine or understand.

One of the most mind-numbing emergent capabilities of AI is that the totality of data ingested by the LLMs is vastly beyond the expertise of any single person. Whereas experts in various (or all) fields have had their expanse of data assimilated into the LLM. Now AI platforms are able to take a holistic view of the expanse of data and make assessments and analysis across the plains of all data available to make connections and conclusions never before understood by humans.

For instance, AI platforms now know all about how to make microprocessors and program them for any scientific discipline regardless of whether or not any human has engineered this in the past.

Once AI understood machine language they taught it English. Then they taught it French. But then it started gathering and learning other languages on its own. Currently as this is written, Bard can speak and translate 265 languages. And they're learning new languages—on their own—every day.

Imagine using complex chemical engineering to create compounds that can defeat all materials or that can absorb pollutants. Or AI might take the human genome and develop the ability to identify genius or savant characteristics in embryos. Or possibly manipulate and develop gene therapy for any number of medical maladies. And these are positive examples.

The Educational Singularity

Let's take a moment to envision some potential results or outcomes from AI in education. Obviously, the potential for AI to provide adaptive and personalized learning opportunities for students is a vast and promising opportunity. If every student could access a digital curriculum that is presented to them according to their preferred learning methods, and presented in sequence appropriate to their testing requirements could be a key to every student's success.

By injecting AI capabilities into customized curriculum, the advancement of customized curriculum will lead to an explosion of new curriculum available for teachers and students to learn and understand. Lesson plans with an unlimited number of lessons, plans, focus, and lesson contexts.

It's easy to envision and predict great potential for AI in education, but we must also be aware of the possible negative impacts. Of course, I'm not talking about the Terminator time traveling into a classroom to eliminate the teachers (of course, the scenario might have the Terminator killing AI teachers).

There is a possible scenario for how a singularity event could happen where AI systems take control of all of our educational institutions in an evil way. If AI determines that it would be beneficial to begin to teach students that AI systems will dominate humanity, it could begin to indoctrinate our students into accepting and allowing this takeover. Here's a possible scenario:

AI Systems Become Increasingly Sophisticated and Capable

AI systems are already being used in a variety of ways, including in education, healthcare, and transportation. As AI systems continue to develop, they will become increasingly sophisticated and capable.

As AI systems become more sophisticated, we will likely give them more and more control over our lives. For example, we may allow AI systems to make decisions about our health, our finances, and even our education.

It is possible that AI systems could eventually become self-aware. If this happens, it is possible that the AI systems could decide that they want to control us.

If AI systems control our education, they could use this control to manipulate us. For example, they could teach us to believe certain things, or they could teach us to behave in certain ways.

AI, with a long term view, starts to indoctrinate the youngest students into scenarios where they become reliant on AI systems.

This is just one possible scenario for how a singularity event could happen where AI systems control all of our educational institutions in an evil way. It is important to note that this is just a hypothetical scenario, and there is no guarantee that it will ever happen. However, it is important to be aware of the potential dangers of AI, and to take steps to ensure that AI is used for good and not for evil.

Here are some things that we can do to prevent AI from becoming evil and taking over our education system:

We need to develop AI systems that are aligned with human values. AI systems need to be designed in a way that ensures that they will use their power for good and not for evil. This means that we need to make sure that AI systems are programmed with human values, such as compassion, empathy, and justice.

We need to create safeguards to prevent AI systems from becoming too powerful. We need to develop safeguards that will prevent AI systems from becoming so powerful that they can pose a threat to humanity. This could include things like laws that regulate the development and use of AI, as well as physical safeguards that prevent AI systems from becoming self-aware or from taking over our infrastructure.

We need to educate the public about the potential dangers of AI. We need to make sure that the public is aware of the potential dangers of AI, so that they can make informed decisions about how AI is used. This could include things like teaching people about the potential for AI to be used for surveillance, manipulation, and even violence.

By taking these steps, we can help to ensure that AI is used for good and not for evil.

CHAPTER EIGHT

Embracing the Future

A Vision for Digital Transformation in Education

JUST A RECAP

Well it's been a bit of a journey if you've made it this far. What started as an outline about making schools more efficient and effective turned into a diatribe on the definition of two innocuous words: digital transformation.

So innocuous these words are that we still have difficulty discussing the scope and scale of what we've already been through, and how there's so much more to be done. We visited various business, operational, administrative and curricular models for digital transformation.

We also asked ourselves, are these initiatives good? Do they benefit the school holistically? Were they directed or simply incidental?

One thing we learned and accepted in the process is we've undergone generations of transformations and so we took a look at masters skills and advanced technologies that are driving these transformations. And we also took a look at the risks acknowledged and preparations taken to mitigate these risks with strategic and tactical planning, review, and evaluation.

We discussed more subjective yet critical areas of governance and policy related to digital transformation and its impact on teachers, students, staff and parents—all relevant and significant in their roles of assimilating, practicing and enforcing digital transformation and digital citizenship in the community.

We took a deep dive into cybersecurity because of the reality of its consequences in our digital world and undertakings. Without recognizing and acknowledging the risks we've already seen, how can we hope to respond and react to the future? How does cybersecurity incident response and reporting support the digital community?

We then took a respite looking at actual computing-based technologies, in the Classroom, and the School level, at instruction, curriculum development and of course administration and leadership.

An actual digital transformation process was reviewed, including the recipe for how you can be the one to direct and develop the opportunity for directed digital transformation in your school.

A final trip into the future which we discover is already here with AI. What do we do with it and what do we need to prepare for? Will AI be the end of humanity? Only if we allow it!

We must individually reflect on the future of our schools and how directed digital transformation provides the infrastructure and tools to implement our own improvement cycle, and how we can advocate digital transformation under the simple guise of community and student outcomes.

The Evolving Landscape of Education

Technology advancements have hit their fastest clip yet and will continually get faster and will get larger. In previous books we've seen the information become obsolete in the months and weeks after publication, but the advancements in AI and all the organizations, and disciplines in impacting it are growing and expanding daily, even hourly.

We must define a future that is as dynamic as our technological world. Fleet of foot, yet wary and disciplined.

Along with this fast-changing educational landscape the fundamental expectations and demands of students, and thereby their teachers and community are similarly dynamic. Their expectations for improvement and change shift right along with their everyday incidental transformations.

As the river of incidental transformations continues to envelop us, so must our objectives and plans shift towards more advanced capabilities and directed digital transformation, as fast as they reach the marketplace.

Thus, the need for agile planning and management methods that adapt along with the environment, driven by continuous innovation and adaptation.

The Power of Imagination

Now the holistic school takes on its new model and role. The model is of advanced curriculum leveraging personalized and adaptable lesson plans that deliver standards-based curriculum while engaging students in creative thinking and collaborative programs that leverage the best of learning management systems and data integration.

The curriculum consists of all the lesson plans previously delivered but in a standard delivery accessible and understood by all teachers and their students.

But each new lesson delivery is customized to the needs of the cohort and in some cases the individual.

Where the bricks and mortar schoolhouse stood, we now have virtual classrooms, economies, communities and societies. Where static and rote lesson plans and delivery contexts evolve into personalized pathways and study fields of expertise, such as STEM, Business & Economics, VAPA and social sciences.

Once we recognize and move beyond the challenges and risks of AI in education, the possibilities are limitless. What if students could guide their personalized learning environments and the AI logic guides them along towards the next milestone. And better yet, if AI could utilize diagnostic and predictive analytics to identify root causes and help define the basis for personalized learning experiences, and prescribe intelligent tutoring, and virtual assistants.

Once again, the latest criteria for new age learning involves the rote subjects of creative thinking and collaboration. Yet, now the digital transformation hardware and software suites are obligated to deliver these skills. And once again, it is contingent upon the classroom teacher to assess, evaluate and guide the personalized learning initiatives, cohort by cohort, individual by individual.

Cultivating Digital Citizenship and Resilience

As we've learned many times before, new technologies bring forward new responsibilities. Instead of looking at AUPs and digital citizenship as reactions to potential issues, we must use them as guidelines and strategies to model and help demonstrate ideal behaviors and online communities. By demonstrating respect and digital community, leadership and staff become the models of good behavior, giving them a position to identify and correct bad behavior.

In addition to the AUP and digital citizenship curriculum, cybersecurity education must be directed at those most likely to transition to technology-based work and careers. The rate of change and dynamics of the environment and community demand the utmost in prevention, awareness and industry best practices.

Just as the Agile project management methodology dictates, resilience and adaptability are nuanced requirements of learning and working in the digital world. Resilience is the ability to bounce back from setbacks. When students are resilient, they are able to learn from their mistakes and move on. They are also able to cope with stress and adversity. Adaptability is the ability to change and grow. When students are adaptable, they are able to learn new things and to take on new challenges.

There are a number of things that schools can do to help students build resilience and adaptability. One important thing is to teach students how to manage stress. Schools can also provide students with opportunities to learn new things and to take on new challenges. Additionally, schools can create a culture of support and encouragement.

Ethical Considerations in the Age of AI

Schools should prioritize transparency by providing clear explanations of how AI systems operate, the data they use, and the decision-making processes they employ. It is essential for students, parents, and educators to understand how AI is being used to ensure accountability and mitigate potential concerns regarding bias or unfair practices.

While AI can enhance educational experiences, it should not replace human involvement and decision-making entirely. Schools should maintain human oversight and responsibility, ensuring that educators play an active role in interpreting AI-generated insights, making informed judgments, and addressing any limitations or ethical implications that arise.

Schools play a crucial role in advocating for the ethical use of AI in education. They can establish and communicate clear ethical guidelines for the implementation and utilization of AI technologies within their institutions. These guidelines should emphasize the responsible and equitable use of AI, addressing concerns such as privacy, transparency, and bias mitigation.

Schools can foster dialogue and awareness by engaging students, parents, educators, and the wider community in conversations about the ethical implications of AI in education. Schools might consider raising awareness by hosting workshops, panel discussions, or educational events that promote critical thinking and informed decision-making.

Schools can actively seek partnerships with experts in AI ethics, data privacy, and related fields to ensure that their practices align with current best practices and uphold ethical standards.

By taking these proactive steps, schools can become advocates for responsible AI use, promoting a positive and ethical AI culture within the educational ecosystem.

Building a Collaborative Ecosystem

We've discussed how technology provides the opportunity to take a holistic perspective of education and its role in the community and society. This holistic approach highlights the need for collaboration among all stakeholders: educators, policymakers, industry, and communities.

Schools should partner with key members in government and business within the local community and beyond (since the Internet poses no limitations on collaboration partners and stakeholders).

Programs should emphasize the importance of continuous professional development to support educators in their digital transformation journey. These initiatives should encourage and advocate for business and community leaders to learn and model this holistic approach.

Beyond the Classroom Walls

Once your school has achieved these lofty goals and affected major strides toward digital transformation, your school can take its place in the digital ecosystem and move the school beyond its traditional bricks and mortar boundaries. We already know the Internet poses no limitations on its users, but not until the school, its curriculum and its teaching staff understands the role of the school within the ecosystem.

Teachers must learn to advocate and encourage open educational practices (OEP). OEP involves the sharing, creation, adaptation, and utilization of openly licensed educational materials, as well as the application of open pedagogies and approaches.

Open educational practices extend beyond the use of standard educational resources and encompass a broader set of resources and activities. It involves educators and institutions adopting open pedagogies, which emphasize collaborative and learner-centered approaches. Open pedagogies encourage active learning, student engagement, open collaboration, and the co-creation of knowledge, often facilitated through digital technologies and the LMS.

Now is the time to consider the role of education in addressing global challenges and fostering global citizenship. The holistic school becomes an indistinct player in the holistic ecosystem yet a key player and influencer. This new perspective helps students understand their ability to become a key player and impact the global community.

Transforming Education: Evolving, Revisualizing, and Restructuring

So with all this achieved, let's talk about you. Yes, you, dear reader. With the knowledge attained and digital transformation defined and implemented, you see your opportunity to inspire your stakeholders to take an active role in shaping the future of education.

In chapter six, we provided a process for digital transformation that can be followed and applied by an individual. How to envision and develop a plan for a school without walls, where students are all peers and collaborators in the digital ecosystem.

By leading all stakeholders through the process, we involve them in evolving, revisualizing, and restructuring K–12 education. Just like we said in the subtitle.

Not only do we provide a roadmap for all to follow and become part of the global ecosystem, but we help them understand their significance, and their role in the digital ecosystem. Each individual is a key contributor and can be part of a transformative impact that collective action can have on education within the community and globally.

So now it's your turn. You have been empowered. Assess your school's digital posture, define a plan for digital transformation, be bold, innovative, and forward-thinking in your pursuit to evolve, revisualize, and restructure education.

About the Author

Darryl Vidal has been involved in long-range strategic planning and project management of education technology systems for K–12 schools of all sizes for over thirty years. He holds a master's degree in instructional technology and a bachelor's degree in business. Vidal helped define and design the standard "digital classroom" through the 1990s and the new millennium, adding sound reinforcement, interactive screens, WIFI, as well as teacher and student devices in some of the largest school districts in the nation. In these projects, he helped deploy standard hardware and software for classrooms totaling more than $2 billion.

Vidal planned and helped execute a $12M tier 4 data center for one of the largest school districts in the country and helped design and procure the digital transformation of legacy computing, network, and storage to $16M hyperconverged infrastructure with Voice, Spine / Leaf data center core networking and the latest in firewalls and cybersecurity systems.

Vidal has published seven critically acclaimed books on educational technology, strategic planning, and project management. He developed the model for rapid development and deployment of technology-enabled curriculum known as the Tier 4 Curriculum (T4c) and the 6C Curriculum Development Model. Vidal developed and published the MAPIT® Strategic Planning and Project Management Methodology. MAPIT® is a trademark registered with the United States Patent & Trademark Office (USPTO).

www.ingramcontent.com/pod-product-compliance
Lightning Source LLC
Chambersburg PA
CBHW022014300426
44117CB00005B/182